D1077419

A Life of Adventure

Lesley Grant-Adamson

faber and faber

LONDON · BOSTON

First published in 1992
by Faber and Faber Limited
3 Queen Square London WC1N 3AU
This open market paperback edition first published in 1992

Printed in England by Clays Ltd, St Ives plc

© Lesley Grant-Adamson, 1992

A CIP record for this book is
available from the British Library

ISBN 0-571-16757-8

2 4 6 8 10 9 7 5 3 1

For Mike and Marion Dent

One

Ambush. A male figure stepped sharply out of shadow to fill the alleyway with its shape. Beyond it neon flashed. Red. Blue. Yellow. Another red for the same danger. Changing light lent it animation but the figure didn't move.

Jim read menace in the silhouette, the angle of the body poised to come for him, its arms held away from the trunk and hands clawing air. He heard the drag of leather on flagstone as his own steps failed. Nervous, he looked over his shoulder. A couple of girls, arm in arm, sauntered past the entrance. Their laughter sang. Nobody had entered the alley behind him.

Retreat, then. Walk, don't run. Running would make the silhouette sure, and Jim had room to hope it wasn't already sure. He walked fast, back the way he'd come, damping down the urge to check how the silhouette had changed, whether it had become a hurtling figure, growing bigger, nearer.

Street sounds engulfed him. Traffic, music, people shouting and a noisy television set in a high-up flat. They destroyed his chance of knowing whether footsteps were throbbing in pursuit. Then, as he joined the street, he succumbed to the backward glance. He saw the red, the blue and the yellow lights. But he did not see the man.

Jim quickened his pace to a trot, in the direction of Piccadilly Underground station, one more young man rushing around London's West End on a warm evening and no one taking notice of him. But when he was held up by traffic lights he spotted a purposeful face approaching from his left. No more room for hope; the man *had* been sure.

Dancing out between cars, Jim escaped across the road and round a corner. People were overflowing from a pub, scenting the air with the sickliness of beer. He eased between them, nudging a glass here and there, unapologetic, intent on a hiding place.

He had the pub lavatory to himself. He shut his mind to the sight of the splash-stained floor, and to the pungent smell of urine mixed with that of frying from the kitchen below. He ran cold water into the basin.

This was the second time he'd been cornered. He couldn't dismiss it as accident, mistake, imaginative interpretation of innocuous behaviour. They were after him.

Frank blue eyes looked back from the mirror unperturbed, telling a lie. He was vain about his fair good looks. He didn't want them marred by a thug in a Soho alley.

The door opened and Jim bent his head, splashing water on his face, avoiding being recognized. Behind him a cubicle door banged, a bolt shot home. Then he went out, found another pub and a telephone. He hesitated, changed his mind about the call. He'd cut free, didn't want to be involved. It had been talk, that was all, but someone – O'Malley or someone – had treated it seriously.

A hand reached over his shoulder, closed around the telephone receiver he was about to relinquish and completed the gesture for him. Jim felt the pressure of a body, intimidating although not exactly touching him. He adopted an expression of puzzlement and turned.

The man was tall and broad, a dog kept on another man's choke chain, who looked as though nothing pleased him more than the command to attack. Jim caught beer on the breath. He maintained his look of surprised innocence.

The man spoke: 'You're Jim, right?' The voice was soft and light, not deep enough for a hefty man.

'Who's asking?' He wanted to move off but the arm that had gone for the telephone was a barrier. Besides, he was uncertain if the man was alone.

Another whiff of beer. 'American, like they said.'

Jim scorned the ease of identification. 'You want an American, take your pick. This town's full of Americans.' The fast

2

beat of the New York accent, automatic choice but a canny one. A don't-mess-me-around kind of accent.

'Tourists.' The word was spat out, something unpleasant. 'It's not a tourist we're looking for, it's you.'

Jim abandoned the pretence of incomprehension. He returned a bleak gaze. The arm that was a barrier dropped, but this didn't signal freedom.

'We're going to walk out of here,' the man said. 'I'm going to be one step behind you all the way. And I'm fast, so don't get any clever ideas.' With a jerk of his head he ordered Jim to the door. The crowd in the bar parted without paying attention to them.

Parked outside was a two-door car, engine running, and a bull-necked driver slamming an impatient fist on the steering wheel. 'Get in,' said the voice behind Jim's right ear. The front passenger seat was already tilted forward for him to squeeze into the back.

Jim tried to concentrate on the route they were taking. He knew parts of London well, most of it not at all. Ten minutes from Soho he could be lost. He kept his eye on the street signs but his thoughts wandered, worrying what would happen when the drive ended and how bad it would be.

Then there was a mews, a back door, a smoky room above an amusement arcade. He'd pictured various things but not the corny business of the boss man dressed like an old-time spiv with a trilby and a cigar. The reality was that the clothes happened to be back in fashion, but the effect was of walking into a time warp, a Cagney film. Apart from that there was nothing to smile about.

He wished he could write them off as small-time riff-raff playing at being in the big time; but they impressed him, troubled him with the extent of their knowledge. They'd got it from O'Malley, of course, and what O'Malley hadn't known he'd invented. Jim calculated they wouldn't like it if he told them they'd been lied to, conned, although one way and another that was true.

He played the slick New Yorker laying out the deal but he angled for time. 'It'll come good, but it's gonna take a while.'

'How long?' The man tipped back the trilby. Piggy eyes screwed up against smoke.

'Weeks. Maybe months.'

'The way O'Malley was talking . . .'

'Sure, but the other guy changed his schedule. There's no way this thing can be pushed.'

The cigar ground out in an ashtray. 'All right, Jim. But I want to know as soon as there's any movement. I don't like freelances, see.' It was all understated, in an English manner Jim had learned not to ignore. So much was left unsaid, his danger implicit.

Jim nodded. 'Right.'

'Time for another ride then.' His eyes had left Jim, the remark was to the others in the room.

The two who'd brought him led him back to the car. 'Where to?' asked the driver.

'Soho's fine.'

The light voice of the big man contradicted. 'Not this time, Jim. We're taking you all the way home.'

Jim guessed they didn't know where he lived, wanted to learn where they could find him in future. Everything they had was attributable to O'Malley, and O'Malley wouldn't know where he lived.

'Kentish Town,' said Jim. It was on his route. Because they'd caught him twice in the West End he credited them with having tried to tail him home. Kentish Town was credible.

When they reached the district he directed them off the main road, and once they entered a street of tall houses carved into flats he told them that was it. The passenger had to get out of the car first and as Jim ducked past him he noticed the fellow studying the façade, memorizing details.

'Top floor,' Jim told him. He walked towards the house, listening for the sounds of the man climbing into the car, the driver preparing to move off. None of those sounds came.

'Jim?' There was warning in the voice.

Jim stopped.

The man said: 'It could be a bad mistake to muck us about. Very bad.'

4

Jim nodded. 'Sure.'

He went on, up a short path, then steps. In the ground-floor flat he saw a handful of young men and women enjoying good-natured argument around a dining table, their sounds suppressed by double-glazing. The car door still hadn't shut. Jim feigned searching for door keys. Beside him was an entryphone. With his body masking action, he jabbed the button for the ground-floor flat while his other hand went on fumbling through jacket and trouser pockets.

Only one of the cards on the entryphone identified the full name of the occupant: Max Minter, flat number 3. A young male voice came over the phone. Jim asked him to open the door, saying he'd been ringing for Max Minter without getting an answer but Max had warned him the bell was unreliable.

Smooth, plausible. It got the street door unlocked. As he stepped over the threshold he heard the car door close and the vehicle grind away. He skipped upstairs, wasted a minute before creeping down again. He shut the front door behind him with the tiniest click.

The railway station was at Kentish Town West. He waited for the train home, standing apart from other passengers on the platform, stance relaxed, hands deep in pockets. He was trembling.

He hadn't been hurt this time. They'd accepted his excuses, *this time*. But the episode had put an end to doubt, his and theirs. They'd looked him over and they hadn't kicked him out. They'd decided they could use him. He'd confirmed O'Malley's story, he'd been given little option but to do that, and he'd acquiesced. That was the worst of it: he'd acquiesced. There'd been a moment to say no, it's a misunderstanding; things have changed; I got it wrong in the first place; or, it'll never work. He hadn't seized that moment. Admiration, implied by their need of him, had kept him silent when he could have altered the future by speaking. Fear had swayed him too. They weren't in the first division but they knew how to be rough. If he'd said those things and they'd chosen to disbelieve him, he could have been in trouble.

5

Instead it had ended with an element of trust between them: they dared not proceed without him and he dared not do so without them. Trust. Risk. It was all the same.

His initial mistake had been to confide in O'Malley, but what else had there been for them to do but talk? Few men would have been rash enough to rely on tales told under those circumstances, but O'Malley had proved tenacious.

And now he would have to lie low, keep clear of central London. All this, while he was working on a scheme that drew him there. He cursed the folly of boasting, cursed O'Malley. The evening's encounters jeopardized everything.

The train was delayed and he cursed that too. There'd been difficulties with the service for weeks. Essential track maintenance, breakdowns, a variety of excuses for keeping people hanging around. When it arrived it was crowded and Jim had to sit with a group of boisterous girls who appraised him beneath mascaraed lashes and giggled their approval. He stared out of the window at dowdy allotments, crumbling factories, and counted the eight stations home.

Willesden, west London, on a Saturday evening in June and a birthday was being celebrated. West Indians eddied around a house thumping with the tempo of reggae. A swivel-hipped girl, high on happiness, tried to inveigle Jim into the house but he joked and disengaged himself. 'Some other time, sister.'

She called enticement after him as he headed up the street, her words chopped off by the cry of an express going through the junction. Trains. Always the presence of trains. One time he used to count each one heard on the walk from the station to his room, but it was as daft as kids counting cracks in pavements. Too many for there to be any point or significance. The express faded and the Trinidadian band reasserted itself.

Jim's room in Tubbs Road was an attic furnished on the beachcomber principle: random objects deposited as erratically as the tide throws flotsam on a beach. His window was at the back. Scrubby gardens, given over to cats and washing

6

lines, stuck out behind the Victorian terrace as if to hold the trains at bay.

He went to the window and watched a three-carriage local slide along the platform of the North London line, the line riding high on stilts above the others. Two more trains were at ground level: a blue and yellow blur tearing away north and a silvery Underground train pulling out of the station.

Jim's door was wide open. He preferred that, knowing he was certain to hear if anyone came. Behind its partition in a corner of his room the cold-water tank rumbled and set pipes groaning, a note that rose to a squeal and faded in a hiss. Then a stair creaked. Jim called: 'Stefan?'

'Is that you, Jim?' That was usually Stefan's greeting.

'Come on up.'

He returned to his window. Stefan paused, as he always did, at the doorway, nervous about encroaching. Nervousness was a major part of Stefan's problem. He was clouded with incomprehension, his face stuck with the expression of a man realizing he's missed the joke. And yet with Jim he felt easy. He hovered, a pathetic figure with his straggling dark hair and his grubby shirt escaping from the waistband of trousers that had been another man's before they'd become Stefan's.

'Come right in,' said Jim, as casually as a man might who has to say the same thing each time the same visitor hesitates.

Stefan looked down to the trains. His own room had a street view. 'Have you seen that HST again? The one with the white roof?'

'No, only that afternoon you were here.'

'I don't get it. Why does InterCity want an HST engine running around in the livery of a Class 43?'

Jim shrugged. 'Maybe somebody preferred the colours.'

'No, they have to stick to . . . Oh, look at this coming down.'

Some empty PGA ironstone hoppers wound through the junction. Then Stefan said: 'When I was a kid I knew a boy who had a train set. A really huge one, I mean.' He was remembering aloud rather than telling Jim a story. 'Steam engines, miles of track and ever so much rolling stock. O gauge, of course. And there were bits of mirror to make the marshalling yard look twice as big as it was, or to kid you the line was going right out through the skirting board. He had it all laid out on the floor in a special room in his house, and he and his dad used to play with it. Really nice.'

'A great way to spend time,' said Jim, injecting enthusiasm. Stefan had mentioned the boy and the train set plenty of times before. He'd never said he'd been allowed to play with it too.

Stefan pushed his shirt back into his waistband. 'I shouldn't think you had one, though. Being in America, I mean. Toys and everything would be different, wouldn't they?'

'I guess it was much the same.' Jim moved round slightly to draw attention away from the massive uncontrollable train set outside.

Stefan swivelled too. Swivelled and remembered. 'Jim, can I ask you about this form?'

He could never make head nor tail of forms, he brought them all to Jim. He'd been careful but even so the paper had snagged along the edges. A few strands of tobacco fell away as Jim unfolded it. Jim considered him a boy, despite the reiteration on the forms that Stefan was twenty-three. Twenty-three, and he wrote like a lazy ten-year-old.

The form was an application for a handout, more precisely for a payment to be waived, and Stefan had filled in parts of it in ungainly handwriting although block capitals were stipulated. Two of the questions had him stumped.

Jim said: 'They're only for people who're already in receipt of this other benefit.' He tapped the form where the words descended into jargon guaranteed to deter deserving petitioners like Stefan. 'We'll put "Not Applicable".'

'Oh, yeah. I thought that was it.'

That was something else he was prone to do, pretend an opinion that hadn't crossed his mind. Covering up his shortcomings, although it required more than that. Jim picked up a ballpoint.

'I've brought the pen,' said Stefan, and drew one from among the fluff in his trouser pocket.

The handwriting was a disgrace, but in his mind what mattered was that the form be completed in the same colour ink and thickness of nib rather than be spoiled or invalidated by a switch.

With Stefan's pen Jim completed the form, adding James Rush and a spurious address where it asked for the signature of a witness.

Stefan took the pen and the form back. He was half-way to the door when he remembered the other thing he had to say to Jim. 'A man came round asking for you.'

'What time?' The news jarred but he concealed this.

'About four o'clock. Yesterday.'

'*Yesterday*?' His casualness was slipping. Yesterday, dammit, and Stefan had said nothing until now.

'I was going to tell you last evening but I forgot.'

'Did the guy say who he was? Or what he wanted?'

A shake of Stefan's head.

'Did he have a car?'

'A blue one, metallic paint. He parked it up the road, by the church.'

Jim tried for a description of the man. All he got was medium height, brown hair and an accent that Stefan hazarded was Scottish.

'If he comes by again,' said Jim, 'don't tell him I'm here but come right on up and let me know he's around. OK?'

'OK,' said Stefan. He hitched his trousers. 'OK, Jim.'

When he was alone again Jim threw up the window and invited in the discordant sounds of trains and party music. He leaned on the sun-warmed stone of the sill, trains swerving below but his eyes on the yellowish evening sky. The scene was at once vital and abandoned, expansive and space-denying. It was painted with the grey of steel rails and scrap yards, an unforgiving, crowded, emptiness with not one single human figure to be seen. Jim watched it for five minutes or so, fascinated by its brutalism, repelled by its sulphurous sunset. Then he closed the sash and drew the curtain.

He switched on the lamp with the forget-me-nots printed on the scorched yellow shade. The lamp was one of the pieces of furniture in the room when he'd taken it. All he'd added was a mirror. He had to have a mirror.

His room was scrupulously neat, unlike Stefan's which contrived to be cluttered when the inhabitant owned next to nothing. Jim hung his cotton jacket in the wardrobe, smoothing it so that it hung free instead of catching on the other garments in there. He adjusted the few hangers until there were equal gaps between each on the rail.

After that he made a mug of instant coffee, took a folder out of a drawer in the chest, and read through newspaper and magazine cuttings. In a while he leaned back in his chair, shut his eyes tight and asked himself questions, silently posed and silently answered. Satisfied, he flipped the folder shut and returned it to the drawer.

He spent Sunday reading the papers, listening to a concert on the radio, watching television and again testing himself on his knowledge of the contents of the manila folder. An uneventful but satisfactory day, forced to do nothing he didn't want to do and enjoying the little he chose.

Peace was destroyed during Sunday night, when he awoke disorientated. He lay rigid and waited for the threat to be clarified. The night was filled with familiar sounds: the swish of trains, a distant police siren, the city's never-ceasing throb of traffic. Yet something had ruptured his dreams and brought him to wary wakefulness.

Then it happened again. A moan, from within the house. Jim reached for the lamp and illuminated the forget-me-nots. He shoved his feet into shoes, turned on the stair light and got as far as Stefan's room before the moan was repeated. The door was locked. Jim's hand spun on the knob. 'Stefan? *Stefan!*'

He took the rest of the stairs two at a time, down to the ground floor and old Geordie who ought to have a key to Stefan's room and certainly had a telephone. Geordie, a man who was consuming his life pint by pint, wasn't roused by the clamour. Jim hared upstairs and kicked open Stefan's door.

Stefan was on the floor, tangled in bed clothes. Jim turned him over to prevent him choking on his vomit, and he moved a chair that was close to his head. And when an indignant Geordie staggered up the lower flight to ask what the hell the noise was about, Jim told him to phone for an ambulance.

He had to tell him twice before Geordie reacted and went away grumbling that he'd have something to say to his sister, who owned the property, about the kind of noisy tenant she'd taken on. Geordie, befuddled, sent for the police and not the ambulance.

'What drugs was he on?' the young constable with the bad skin asked Jim. 'They're usually on something, they can control epilepsy these days.'

Jim was irritated by the insensitivity. Stefan didn't control much else in his life, how could anyone assume he'd control an illness? But all he said was: 'He never mentioned it.'

'Came as a bit of a shock, then?' said the other police officer. 'Waking up at dead of night to all this.'

'All this' meant the disordered room (he wasn't to know that Stefan always lived in disorder), the animal indignity, and Jim's own unsought responsibility to deal with it. Jim shrugged. He'd encountered worse.

He turned down an invitation to go to the hospital in the ambulance. He was a neighbour, a form-filler, but he couldn't afford to be elevated to close friend. 'I'll call by and check on him in the morning,' he said. 'They can tell him that, when he comes round.'

Geordie was foul-tempered once the ambulance had gone. 'See here,' he said, stamping about the passage in his bare feet, 'there's a broken door to be accounted for. I've keys to the doors, you know, for emergencies. That lad falling down in a fit was an emergency and you were to come to me for a key. Who's going to explain to my sister about the door, that's what I want to know?'

'I'll take care of it, Geordie.' Jim pushed by him.

Geordie continued as though the offer had never been made. 'You lads are all the same, think you can carry on anyhow and leave my sister to pick up the bills.'

Jim climbed the stairs, Geordie's complaint unrelenting. By Stefan's room he faltered, sniffed the acrid air and opened

11

a window before shutting the door on the mess. Two minutes later he was back in bed and chasing sleep.

The wind had changed and threw the cacophany of trains louder against his window. Far-off wailing of a police car was transformed in his dream into an ambulance dodging through the West End with him in the back being held down by two policemen. He awoke nervy and unrested.

Although he was due at work at nine, he squeezed in a visit to the hospital first. Stefan was all right, exhausted but all right. He asked after Geordie, fretting about what the old man might report to his sister.

Jim assured him that he was going to call on the landlady himself that evening. 'It'll be fine,' he said. 'Don't worry about it.'

Stefan nodded, unconvinced. Then: 'People don't like . . .'

'It'll be fine.'

Rain was falling as he walked from Acton station and along drab side roads to the office. This was at the rear of the shop and he usually reached it from a yard where the vans pulled in, but as he was late the shop was open so he went in that way. The shop was in an old-fashioned terrace of urban clutter, brave fascias and failing businesses. Next door had been empty for years, its boarded window thick with fly posters for long-gone rock concerts and forgotten demos.

He nodded a good morning to pernickety Eric Shaw, the deputy manager, and winked at the assistant whom Shaw was ticking off. But he had time only to scan the job list before Shaw followed him into the office. 'Late again, Jim.'

Jim detested him but had never done anything to reveal it. He said: 'Sorry, Eric, I had to go to the hospital. The Hodges' house this morning, isn't it?'

Jim had headed off the cutting remarks he'd prepared, so all Shaw could say was: 'Er . . . Yes, the Hodges. But don't think you can take all day over it.'

'Looks pretty straightforward.' Jim helped himself to the keys of one of the vans. He gathered up the equipment and drove off before Shaw could find an opportunity to needle him.

It was one of Jim's Monday-morning fantasies that he

would take over the business and sack Eric Shaw. But he would pick on him first. He would mock Shaw's silly hairstyle with its wedge of greying hair brushed across the crown to conceal baldness. He would point out that a pin-striped suit was indeed appropriate for work but that shirt collars so battered they flipped up instead of curving down were slovenly. He'd nag about Shaw's scuffed and unshiny black lace-ups. And he'd oblige Shaw to keep his nasty observations about his colleagues to himself. Also he'd cast doubts on Shaw's honesty by querying his stock-taking methods. In other words, he'd do nothing to Shaw that Shaw didn't every day of the week do to his subordinates.

Jim drove to the Hodges' house and set about installing a satellite television dish. Most shops sent fitters round in pairs, which was quicker and safer, especially when it came to using ladders, but Eric Shaw didn't appreciate the advantages and Jim worked solo. Mr and Mrs Hodges had requested that their dish be hidden on the roof at the back but this wasn't possible if the equipment was to receive a signal. Jim set about fixing it to the right of the front-bedroom window.

An excitable woman from across the road alerted Mrs Hodges. Soon they were all in the kitchen while an attempt was made to telephone Mrs Hodges's husband. Jim talked the women out of calling Eric Shaw. It wasn't that he was unsympathetic to Mrs Hodges, a dumpy woman who liked her 1970s neo-Georgian the way it was and believed an imitation coach lamp was all the adornment required; but if the household was to have a dish there was no better position for it than the front wall.

'The man who came before was *absolutely sure* it would be all right on the roof at the back,' repeated Mrs Hodges.

Jim didn't react. It wouldn't do to spell out that the salesman had lied for the sake of securing the sale. Mrs Hodges was told that her husband was out of the office and she rang off. 'We-ell,' she said, and pulled with pudgy fingers at her lower lip.

The neighbour chimed in. 'I'd speak to the shop, Phyllis. I mean, after all, things should be done the way the customer wants them done.'

'Look, Mrs Hodges,' said Jim, wishing the other woman would go home and worry about her own affairs instead. 'Why don't I finish putting the dish by the window now that I've started? If you aren't happy with the reception, and you still think it would be better round the back, then we can move it in a week or two.'

'We-ell.' She was weakening nicely.

The neighbour challenged the notion that it would take that amount of time for them to make up their minds about the quality of the reception. And Jim claimed that the shop had such a lot of business that there was no possibility of coming back earlier.

By the time he was back up the ladder the rain he'd left behind in Acton had pursued him to Ealing. He hurried through the outside work, demonstrated the television set for Mrs Hodges and secured her signature as proof that the equipment was working. The rest, he reasoned, was between the Hodges ménage and Eric Shaw.

He stopped at a pub for lunch. Shaw's instructions were that the men were to telephone the office once they completed jobs, but it suited them not to. Avoiding it, or delaying, denied him control. Everyone – fitters and shop assistants – resented his manner, which had become worse since he'd been in charge during the manager's prolonged illness. The boldest undermined his authority as hard as he fought to establish it.

Lunch over, Jim browsed in a newsagent's and carried a copy of *Time* back to the van. He studied one particular article and, as he drove on, he asked himself questions and supplied answers from memory. Once, when an answer wouldn't surface, he swung the van into a lay-by, looked up the feature and checked a point. The solution didn't please him. 'Discrepancy,' he murmured. 'Can't both be right.' Then he continued the journey quizzing himself over and over until he reached Acton.

Eric Shaw went on the attack, his clump of grey hair quivering. Mrs Hodges had rung. Jim, said Shaw, had countermanded instructions and created a dissatisfied customer. 'We're here to give good service to our customers, not dictate

14

to them. If she wants her satellite dish on the roof, that's where it should go.

Jim cast his eyes heavenwards and flung the van keys on their hook with a contemptuous gesture. This infuriated Shaw, who would have liked the keys to miss the mark, and he boomed on about Jim's unsuitability to be an installer of satellite dishes for as reliable a local firm as J. and J. Electrical and all that name meant in Acton. 'We have a reputation to maintain but you seem to think you can go into people's homes and do as you like. No wonder there have been complaints. Don't imagine this is the first time.'

The shop staff tuned in to the row and prayed that no customers would drift in from the street and distract them. They heard Shaw going on and on, rising, falling only to rise again. Eventually, when they had begun to wonder whether Jim hadn't walked out of the back door and left Shaw to rant alone, they heard his voice. Tight, controlled, actually quiet. But frightening.

'Don't risk another word.'

The contained threat shut Shaw up. There was nothing more to listen to until the papery sounds of someone getting records up to date or turning the pages of the desk diary, everyday activities carried out without rancour. Shortly, they heard an equally uninteresting routine telephone call, the back door opening and closing and a man's diminishing steps. Everything was back to normal, except that they were left with the impression that Eric Shaw had been poking a snake with a stick while mistaking it for a worm. Sunny Jim, as some of the women called him because of his smiling face, had his dark side.

In between showers Jim did two jobs that afternoon, one of them rectifying an installation carried out by a colleague. That, he knew, was what most rankled with Eric Shaw: he was efficient. Shaw himself hadn't a clue how to go about an installation: he was scared of heights and incapable of offering potential customers sensible advice. He had learned about television and audio equipment over the years and was useful in the shop, but the newer side of the business was beyond him.

15

Jim, on the other hand, had picked it up in no time. He had a facility for picking things up. He shrugged off Shaw's unpleasantness. The fool wouldn't be a problem much longer.

At the first address that afternoon, a teenager, out of work and hanging around his parents' house watching chat shows and videos, took a detailed interest and they shared a cup of tea while Jim satisfied his curiosity about the satellite business. At the second house he met a night-worker who wanted the service despite the misgivings of his wife who muttered suspicions about erotic material being beamed at their children. Jim smoothed the friction, amused them with anecdotes.

Then he pointed the van back to Acton. Eric Shaw was sulking, refusing to acknowledge his arrival although when Jim flipped the van keys on to the hook with another of his negligently precise throws, Shaw couldn't avoid wriggling his shoulders in irritation.

There were three vans. Jim's was the second to return. He strolled across the yard as the third one came in and he stood by the driver's door. Alex was the youngest of the fitters, a streetwise lad with a swagger and jeans that might have been painted on.

'Hi, Alex. What do you have then?' Jim pretended to peer into the back of the van.

'Lay off, Jim.' Laughing, but he flicked a glance towards the office. 'I only said it would be easy.'

'And that you'd love to see Eric's face if you did it.'

'Yes, well, I didn't, did I? Shove over, I want to get out.'

Jim let him open the door. In the corner of his eye Jim was aware of Shaw, impotent at his desk by the window, being encouraged to imagine collusion. Jim clapped Alex on the shoulder. 'I'm off. See you tomorrow.'

'Cheers, Jim.'

But when Jim was nearly out of the yard, in good time for the train home, he was called back.

In the office Shaw said: 'We're missing a dish, Jim. From the Dawson job.'

'No, we're not, Eric. The dish issued for that job's on the side of the Dawson house. I put it there myself.'

Shaw's smile was triumphant and spurious. 'According to the paperwork two dishes went to that house. You took the second one and were to replace the first one. Faulty, I imagine.'

'No, Eric. I couldn't finish the job the first time I went over there because the dish wasn't on the van.'

Shaw's smile tightened a notch. 'Fell off the back of the van, no doubt.'

He got a mocking Southern drawl. 'My, that's an ugly thing to say.'

'There's a dish unaccounted for,' snapped Shaw. He pushed two pieces of paper at Jim, dispatch notes detailing items supplied for the Dawson job. One listed dish, cable, brackets, all the usual items. The other, dated a day later, mentioned only a dish.

Jim brushed the papers aside. 'That proves nothing, except that I called there twice.' Immediately he regretted that phrasing, the undesirable element of challenge. Tantamount to saying: 'Prove it.'

Shaw was supercilious as he smoothed the notes and laid them on the desk. 'It's all the proof I require. Now then, Jim, where's the missing dish?'

An open-handed shrug.

Shaw said: 'Very well. I suggest you think about it overnight. It's not the first time, is it? But on this occasion I know exactly who's responsible for what we euphemistically call our shrinkage.'

Jim shook his head with impatience and walked past him. 'I have a train to catch.' On the way out he tried but failed to meet Alex's eye.

The yellow-brick railway station was in sight before Jim had dissuaded himself from walking out of the job there and then. Shaw's unjustified accusation exceeded anything he'd done before, but leaving in anger would appear to confirm Shaw's opinion of him.

Jim had been employed there three months and lived in Tubbs Road for the same length of time. Both were tolerable

17

only because he'd set a limit. Quite soon, when the moment he was waiting for came, he'd vanish.

The platform was crowded, the train late. Occasionally an announcement, by a man with his lips too close to the microphone for clarity, added more minutes to the delay. Passengers progressed from sympathetic looks to fractious remarks. Jim sensed his old restlessness revive, the urge to be up and off and achieving what he needed instead of being held back, blocked, thwarted by other people's inadequacy and incompetence.

The train was fifteen minutes late. In his head he composed acerbic complaints to the area manager. This was an open-faced intelligent-looking man who smiled out from a poster half-way down the platform. 'If you need help or have any comments about our service, please contact him or one of his team,' it said beneath the photograph. The name was Matthew Reynoldes.

At the house he was confronted by Geordie, fired with the news that five minutes earlier he'd refused entry to Stefan who'd been brought from hospital by ambulance. 'I told them to get the lad away some place he can be looked after. It's not right to put someone like that in here, never knowing what he's going to do next.'

Jim hadn't imagined the hospital sending him home so soon, and he knew without asking that the room hadn't been seen to.

Geordie picked up the thought. 'That room of his, it's a stinking hell-hole. The way some people live!'

'He was nauseous,' Jim said patiently. And when Geordie looked vague, he sought an alternative. 'He was sick, Geordie.'

'Disgusting,' was all Geordie said.

Geordie, thought Jim, managed to be fairly disgusting himself, what with his days spent drinking, his confused evenings and his uncared-for flat where he slumped into snoring sleep. No doubt there were neighbours who thought Geordie also ought to be taken away to be cared for.

The furniture in Stefan's room was speckled by rain that had come through the window opened in the night. Holding his breath Jim bundled up blankets and sheets, then commandeered dustbin bags from a reluctant Geordie.

'Where're you going to dump them?' Geordie asked.

'At the launderette.' Jim surprised him with the idea that anything in the room could be salvaged.

May, a neat woman with red hands, did laundry for people who couldn't wait, but Jim put the stuff into the machines himself rather than let her discover the state it was in. She knew him, he went to the place once a week.

'You don't want to bother yourself, Jim. I'll see to it,' said May, drying fingers on her overall.

But he was already closing the door on the medley of elderly blankets with unravelling hems. 'You take them out and get them dried, OK?'

'See you later, love.'

He hoped it would be all right, that there wasn't something special you were supposed to do when bedding was as soiled as that heap was.

Black youths with cans of Red Stripe in their fists were lounging outside houses as he waited for the bus that carried him to Kensal Green and Geordie's sister. On the way, Jim modified the complaint to Matthew Reynoldes. It didn't stipulate the fate that had befallen Stefan as a result of the delay but it was a firm case for making the trains run on time.

Geordie's sister, Margery Mallinson, was a woman who kept herself tidy, had her hair permed regularly and wore court shoes in the house as well as out of it. An unlikely sister for Geordie. If there was a Mr Mallinson or anyone else at the address, then Jim never knew it. Mrs Mallinson would have conducted business with him on the doorstep, if her patch-eyed terrier hadn't attempted to slip between her legs.

'You'd better come in, Jim,' she said. And in the softly shadowed hall with its decorative moulding: 'My brother telephoned and told me all about the disturbance. The way I see it, a lad that's wrecking his room and having the police round in the early hours has no right to expect to carry on living under the same roof as respectable folk.'

She came up to Jim's shoulder, her head tilted and grey eyes exaggerated behind thick spectacles. Jim smiled down at her. 'Well, now . . .'

'Believe me, Jim, I understand what you've had to put up with and I'm sure if I'd had any idea he was going to be a trouble and a trial I wouldn't have taken him in. I'll have a carpenter put the door right and I'll speak to the Social Services. They ought to be able to find a place he can go.'

'Stefan isn't a problem. He was ill one night, that's all.'

The eyebrows rose above the rim of the glasses. 'Oh?'

Inch by inch, he raised Mrs Mallinson's sympathy for Stefan. He exuded charm and good sense and prevailed on her to do likewise. He undid the damage Geordie had done. When he left it was with the promise that she'd speak to her brother again.

Stefan was delivered to Tubbs Road next day before Jim left for work. Geordie didn't attempt to bar him although the old man was sullen and gave Stefan to understand that, purely in the lad's own interest, his stay was temporary and the Social Services department was seeking a new berth for him.

Jim missed his train and the next one was cancelled. While he waited he polished the wording of his complaint to the area manager. Eric Shaw became the catalyst that changed this harmless word game into action. By disbelieving Jim's excuse about the cancelled train and resurrecting the accusation of stealing the satellite dish, Shaw provoked Jim to snatch up the telephone and demand to speak to Matthew Reynoldes. The man wasn't available so, using the office typewriter, he pounded out his anger and mailed it.

Shaw said: 'Jim, when you've quite finished playing secretaries, there's the small matter of an installation in South Acton. If, that is, you have any intention of doing any work for us today.' Shaw had allotted this job while Jim was typing, there had been nothing for him when he'd begun.

On the way back from South Acton he noticed a J. and J. van in a pub car park and he pulled in beside it. Alex was having lunch by the fruit machine in the bar. Seeing Jim he looked sheepish, wiped a palm down the skin-tight thigh of his jeans.

'OK,' said Jim with a touch of laid-back California, 'where did Eric Shaw's dish stray to?'

'It wasn't me.' Alex picked up his glass and swaggered over to the table where he'd flung his jacket. Jim followed.

'Your auntie's house? Your granma's?'

'Lay off,' said Alex, but half-hearted.

'You've got your lines wrong,' Jim told him, not unkindly. 'Don't you ever watch television? You're supposed to say it's a fair cop or I've got you bang to rights, or . . .'

'Lay *off*.'

'Not until you make a full confession.' He was enjoying himself.

'I'm saying nothing.'

'This is going to cost you a pint. And when you've paid for it, I'm going to tell you what to do if you *really* want to bug Shaw.'

Alex's eyes widened. 'Yeah?'

'A pint,' Jim repeated.

Alex heard the outline with lip-licking attention. Then he asked: 'But will that work?' He wanted to believe it, dared not.

'Sure,' promised Jim. 'Think about it. But don't ever say where you got the inspiration.'

'Of course not.' A pause, then: 'Jim, you're a genius.'

Jim emptied his glass. 'Could be.' He got up to leave. 'See you later, Alex.'

He left Alex feeding coins into a fruit machine. Jim's own gambling was more sophisticated. Higher stakes, higher risks. The idea he'd just put into Alex's head was several degrees brighter than sneaking the occasional piece of equipment off a van and letting a colleague carry the blame. Jim didn't know whether Alex would have the nerve to see it through or whether imagining he knew a way to circumvent

Shaw would be enough for him. Jim was unconcerned, he wasn't going to be around to find out.

Jim was never without a plan and his plans always centred on a gamble. Someone, a woman, had said so once, although fogged by psychobabble. She'd intended to startle and had met confirmation. She was a psychiatrist, or was she a psychologist? Either way, she'd chirruped jargon, empty of meaning but impressive for all that. Then she'd come down to it: 'You gotta look this thing right in the face, Jim – you have a gambling nature.'

She'd hoped to make it seem unworthy, reprehensible, a condition that led the wise to support groups in search of weapons to combat it. She hadn't appreciated the excitement. Shortly after that conversation they'd stopped seeing each other. He'd missed their talks, her quest for his true nature and his cunning in teasing information from her. Close about her own feelings, her guard slipped once in a while and then he confirmed her depressing lack of originality. Her metaphor for life was a journey interrupted by incidents much as a bus ride is interrupted by bus stops. His, although he withheld this from her, was of a series of junctions where opportunities and alternatives were on offer and he made his choices and rode his luck on lots of little journeys in lots of different directions.

By the end of the week Matthew Reynoldes had sent Jim no reply. Jim felt slighted. Concise and cogent, he didn't deserve to be dismissed as a crank. On Saturday he composed a follow-up letter, coupling the complaints in the first with waspish remarks about Reynoldes's failure to deal with protests from the travelling public.

For the first time since he'd moved to Tubbs Road he didn't go to the West End at the weekend, fearing the men who'd trapped him the previous Saturday. He filled time at the cinema, read, studied the cuttings to which he'd added the article ripped from *Time*, listened to *Jazz FM* and dawdled, arms on his warm window sill, watching the trains go by.

Four times Stefan called out: 'Is that you, Jim?' and came up to talk, hesitating by the door for the routine invitation to enter. Jim soothed Stefan's worries, or attempted to, although Stefan was no longer to be reassured by words. No wonder, because Jim's easy confidence that everything would work out fine was countered by Geordie's sniffing disapproval of Stefan and whatever peculiarities he might perform. And it was impossible for Jim to argue against Stefan's conviction that Geordie was campaigning to have him evicted. Geordie had stated the fact to each of them.

Frustrated, bored, Jim ached with the need to put this wretchedness behind him. He'd lived frugally while working in Acton and managed to save, not much because the job didn't pay much, but sufficient to give him the start he needed. His research was complete, he was primed to go but obliged to delay. Timing depended on someone else and his own move had to dovetail because otherwise the game was lost before it had begun.

Down below the trains flew, crying their urgency. Jim was imprisoned, watching the sun bring a final glimmer of life to scrapyards of cars twisted in metallic *rigor*. He gazed left, in the general direction of what he couldn't see but knew, that other prison, the brick towers of Wormwood Scrubs rearing from the wasteland.

Matthew Reynoldes's reply came on Monday, a pre-printed letter that went none of the distance to answering Jim's points and didn't amount to apology either. Jim telephoned to object to being brushed off but again Reynoldes wasn't free to speak to him. He posted his second letter, tailoring the version that had run through his mind over the weekend so that it covered his annoyance at being sent a standard letter.

Keyed up yet compelled to inactivity, he was letting the Reynoldes business niggle him. Normally he'd have relegated Reynoldes's letter to the rubbish bin and forgotten the affair. As it was, he had nothing better to occupy him. Unfortunately for Matthew Reynoldes he wasn't going to let it drop.

Twice every day Jim sat in trains that pulled alongside platforms where the poster of Reynoldes was displayed. When he arrived at or left Willesden station he walked past

one. The man who'd initially appeared open-faced and intelligent now looked smug. The telephone number offering a
considerate response to customer dissatisfaction seemed a
patronizing trick.

Jim studied Matthew Reynoldes's face and wondered
about the man.

Two

He went to Matthew Reynoldes's house. Eric Shaw had sent
him to carry out work in Kew and when that was finished Jim
took his curiosity about Reynoldes a stage further. Instead of
turning back to Acton he drove the extra few miles to Richmond and set about finding Queens Road.

Discovering that Reynoldes lived in Richmond had been
easy. The telephone directory had offered two possibilities.
When he'd dialled the second of the numbers a woman had
confirmed that it was Matthew Reynoldes's home. After a
few more days without a reply to his letter, he'd decided to
bypass Reynoldes's office. He rang the number again. The
same woman answered that her husband was out. Jim had
dropped the idea, the Kew job revived it.

Well before he located the house he was envying Reynoldes. But after so much appealing period property the
Reynoldes house was a let-down: a 1980s affair, although in
a fine position at the top of the hill and close to both Sheen
Common and Richmond Park.

It stood back from the road, across a courtyard behind a
high wall, and this made it impossible for him to see through
the windows. The garage was open, a new runabout tucked
in one corner. Jim watched from over the road, where there
were no houses but the boundary of a hotel garden. He saw
a beech tree dappling pink brick and a sparrow floating down
to a gatepost.

He shrugged. Finding the house was a pointless achieve-
ment. Unless, that is . . . He darted through the gateway,
up four steps beneath a portico and rang the bell. A woman
opened the door. He asked for Matthew Reynoldes.

'I'm sorry, he's not home,' she said. 'Oh dear, it's too bad, isn't it? He knew very well you were coming.'

She was a good-looking forty, dressed in that low-key English middle-class way: smudgy colours that weren't exactly green and weren't exactly brown. On the telephone her voice had been cool, but face to face she was kinder. Jim put on an expression of rueful disappointment, then said never mind, what did it matter after all?

He left her the initiative and she took it. 'Why don't you come in for a moment? Perhaps he won't be much longer.' She read the time on a chunky gold wrist-watch. Hairs on her arm shone gingery in the sunlight, her skin was pale and lightly freckled.

They went into a sitting room that opened on to the type of garden that implies a team of gardeners lurking behind the shed ready to stamp on any weed that dares.

She said: 'I suppose *I* could show you, except that . . .'

The sound of feet clumping downstairs distracted them. The door was thrown back and a girl, a blonde cuddly girl in a track suit, stood there, mouth open with a remark. Instead, she said: 'Oh.'

Jim gave her his friendly smile, the one that was good at making everything all right. She grinned back. Then, to her mother: 'Must dash, Mummy. I won't be late.'

She bobbed out of sight as she added a goodbye. Her mother called after her: 'Penny, get someone to bring you back, darling. I don't want you wandering around alone.'

Penny grunted what might have been assent. The front door thudded. Mrs Reynoldes and Jim exchanged smiles that spoke amply of the impatience of the very young.

'Tennis,' she said. 'She's going through all the phases. You know, the badminton and the squash and now she's back to good old tennis. Actually, she's quite good at it, even a cautious mother has to admit that.'

'Where does she play?' Jim was visualizing pretty Penny Reynoldes in a tiny skirt, leaping and stretching for a ball.

Her mother mentioned a park.

He said: 'Popular courts, aren't they?' A fair guess, in hot weather all tennis courts were.

'Very, but she's been fortunate. She's played a couple of evenings a week all summer.' She looked at her watch again. 'Oh dear. Perhaps I ought to show you after all.' She stepped into the garden, Jim following.

A few yards out on the lawn the woman swung round. But not, as he thought, to face him with the realization that she'd made a mistake. Her eyes weren't on him at all, they were on the back of the house. She said: 'You see, we thought it would be very nice to have it up there. And then we began to question whether it would be wise to put it on that wall.'

He fished for clues. 'What alternatives did you discuss?'

She was looking his way now, but he kept gazing up at the wall of the house. 'Well none, really. I mean, that's the window of the master bedroom so it would have to go there if it goes anywhere.'

'Of course,' he said quickly.

'Actually we'd rather like it done before the summer ends. It would be such a shame not to, although we do realize that might be asking a bit much.'

'Not necessarily.' He was no nearer enlightenment.

The absurdity struck him, all he could think of was getting away. Not only was Matthew Reynoldes expected at any second but so was the man the Reynoldeses wanted to show the back of the house. Jim did what Mrs Reynoldes had done, made a show of looking at his watch and reacting to the time. 'I have to go, Mrs Reynoldes. I have to meet with someone. Sorry I've missed your husband, but I'll be in touch.'

She apologized for her absent husband, all the way through the garden to the side gate where she let him out into the courtyard beneath the beech tree.

Jim jumped into the office van, high with the thrill of the escapade. He had learned a lot, met the man's charming wife and teenage daughter, and gained an unfavourable impression of Reynoldes's treatment of them. Not once during her apologies had Mrs Reynoldes suggested her husband's failure to be there when required was unusual.

Then he drove up Queens Road, to pass the house and head down Richmond Hill. A red car shot into the courtyard.

Jim slowed and saw Matthew Reynoldes emerge from it, flustered, composing himself in the moment before he let himself indoors.

The man's palpable agitation interested Jim. He speculated about it as he drove on, until a sign caught his eye and he made a slight detour. The tennis courts were busy, groups of youngsters stood around watching the luckier ones play. Penny Reynoldes was one of the lucky ones but she was about to lose, forced all over the court by a superior player. Yet Penny had spirit, she refused to throw the game away. Unobserved, Jim watched her lose the first set.

Next day Alex mentioned having seen, he thought, a satellite dish poked away behind boxes in a corner of the stock room. Jim pretended not to hear but Eric Shaw remarked that if Alex wasn't sure perhaps he'd better *make* sure and then they would know whether or not he had anything to tell. He handed Alex the key to the store.

Alex rolled his eyes and went upstairs. Unoccupied, Jim wanted to go through to the shop and watch the television but Shaw hated it when staff did that. He lectured them on the lines of: 'It gives our customers a very poor impression if the first thing they see when they look in is idle people gawping at the television.' Jim was obliged to stay where he was and await Alex's return.

He'd guessed what Alex was up to, and that he was doing it because Shaw hadn't stopped sniping about the dish Jim was accused of stealing. Jim wished only that Alex could be better at it. That announcement about a dish behind the boxes was the most stagy, unconvincing bit of deception Jim had listened to in a long time.

Alex reappeared, pleased with himself and carrying a dish. 'Here you are, Eric. A dish.'

Shaw was withering. 'Quite so, Alex. I think we can agree on that point. Definitely a dish.' Gradually Shaw moved his eyes from the dish in Alex's hands to meet his eyes.

Jim thought: 'Shut up, Alex. Don't push it.'

Alex pushed it. 'It must have fallen down there or something.'

Shaw pursed his lips. 'Or something? What might that be, I wonder?'

'Look,' said Alex, petulant now and setting the dish down with a bonk on Shaw's desk. 'I've found the bloody thing for you. I'm not going to give you its history too, now am I?'

Shaw picked up the dish and twirled it. 'Down behind the boxes, you say?'

'Yes, come and see.'

'Oh, I hardly need to go grovelling behind the boxes, especially now there's nothing to be seen. Unless, of course, you happened to notice quantities of other escaped stock down there?'

'No!'

'Hmm.' Shaw considered the errant dish. 'And what do you suggest is the significance of this dish being where it was?'

'We were missing a dish, right?'

Shaw countered. 'Weeks ago, Alex, and this one's very clean. I would expect one that had been lying in a disregarded corner for weeks to be extremely dusty.' He looked Alex in the face again. Alex chose to stare at the dish instead.

'I wiped it over when I got it out,' he lied.

Shaw put the dish on the desk and stroked the side of his nose with a finger. 'Well, thank you, Alex. Now the Gunnersbury job, if you would, please.'

Alex coloured, took his van keys off the hook, looked bewildered. Jim winked at him as he left.

He was sorry Alex had made a hash of it. Sorry because it was certain to revive Shaw's accusations of theft and sorry because it meant Alex lacked the wit to succeed with the scam Jim had outlined to him as a way of getting revenge on Shaw. 'A pity,' Jim thought. 'After today's failure he's less likely to attempt it.'

Shaw snapped: 'It's new stock, this dish.'

'I know that,' said Jim.

Shaw brushed an imaginary speck off the sleeve of his worn pin-striped jacket. 'The missing Dawson dish was from a batch we received before they were modified.'

'Yes.' Jim waited.

The man's face contorted in disgust. 'You may think I'm a fool, you no doubt misled Alex, but believe me I'm not to be fobbed off with this thing.' And here he slapped a hand on the dish, making it ring the unmusical note of a badly made bell.

He was a preposterous little man. Jim struggled not to laugh at him but the effort produced an unfortunate smirk. 'I wouldn't expect you to be fooled, Eric.'

Shaw jerked his chin up, the band of hair pasted over his crown flapped. He was saying something about an insult to his intelligence, but Jim made a gesture of helplessness and went into the shop, unable to keep a straight face. He knew he'd be safe in there, he'd heard the doorbell ping seconds earlier. An elderly woman was at the counter buying light-bulbs and she was unwittingly preventing Shaw boiling over. If she gained a poor impression of J. and J. Electrical because Jim was lounging against a washing machine and watching television with a silly smile on his face, she didn't let on.

He wanted to quit. He wasn't truly watching the set, he was simply facing that way while he argued with himself whether he couldn't justify giving notice and leaving there and then. Lately the temptation to resign and escape Shaw had kept flaring up. Shaw had always been malicious but since he'd latched on to the idea that Jim had stolen a dish, he'd persisted in accusing him of theft. Obliquely, sometimes overtly. Jim was weary of the whole set-up.

For weeks he'd been living day to day, bored, uncertain how much longer the phase would last. Life was at another of those junctions, his direction was going to switch. He loathed waiting. But patience was crucial, a move at the wrong moment and months of preparation would go to waste.

'Hold *on*,' he urged himself. 'Don't blow it. Just hold on a little longer.'

The installation job was wide ranging and flexible, it had suited him to take it while he was working up the new scheme. Also, it could protect him from a few of the risks that lay ahead, provide an alibi when he might need one.

The customer left clutching her light-bulbs. In the office the telephone rang. Shaw barked Jim's name. Minutes later Jim was on his way to a flat in South Acton and the pressure was lifted.

Afterwards he broke a habit and rang the office. Daphne, one of the women in the shop, answered and said Shaw was in the washroom but that there was a job to be done near Kew. 'Give me the address, I'll go right over,' said Jim and that way dodged Shaw for the rest of the day.

From Kew, where he advised a man who was wondering whether he would get reliable reception from equipment on the back of his garage, Jim made for Richmond. He liked the long hill, the open views, the skein of the river Thames. Parking where he could join a path through steep gardens, he strolled along the sunlit river bank. He went further than he'd intended, lured on by interesting sights.

Inevitably, his thoughts circled around Matthew Reynoldes who had the good fortune to live in this affluent and pretty river town. For the second time he went to Queens Road. He approached the house through the park, scrutinizing the back of it and wondering what Mrs Reynoldes wanted to fix there but feared would be unwise. Round in the street he saw that elegant urns of geraniums had appeared either side of the portico.

He found a callbox. Mrs Reynoldes again told him that her husband was out. Jim said he'd try later and rang off without leaving a name. He started to drive out of town and he didn't ring again. He didn't need to because he saw Matthew Reynoldes.

Reynoldes's red car dodged in front of him on a round-about and Jim swung after him. Unless Reynoldes knew a short cut, he wasn't heading for home. Neither was he alone. A woman with coiled hair sat beside him.

The pair drove into a car park, leaving Jim uncertain at the entrance. Reynoldes leaned across and the couple kissed. Then the woman got out, the red car spun round to leave and the woman unlocked a blue hatchback. Jim's interest switched to her.

He dogged the hatchback over the bridge and through

Twickenham until it parked in a side street and the driver entered a Victorian cottage. Jim had a clear view of her then. She was younger than Mrs Reynoldes, auburn haired, slim and well dressed in a way that suggested a professional career.

Reynoldes's habitual lateness, his unreliability in family matters were easily accounted for. A mistress took time and that had to be stolen from other relationships. Jim was surprised at the strength of his anger at the man's faithlessness. None of his business how Reynoldes conducted his private life, and yet Jim couldn't shake off that anger. He liked Mrs Reynoldes very much and Reynoldes was hurting her. His contempt for the man increased with every discovery.

Jim fantasized about challenging Reynoldes. He wanted Reynoldes to squirm, to be humiliated and forced to take notice of something other than his own selfish interests. A couple of evenings later Jim checked on the blue hatchback in the car park and hung around until Reynoldes and his girlfriend arrived and drove away in their separate cars. He allowed Reynoldes time to get home and then headed for Queens Road.

Matthew Reynoldes opened the door himself. He was in a foul temper. 'You'll have to wait, I'm on the phone,' he said without preliminaries. And left Jim on the doorstep, studying him. The man's face was harder than on the posters. His hair was thinning over the crown, there were anxiety lines around his eyes and the voice was harsh.

'Yes, I dare say,' said Reynoldes down the line, 'but the point is . . . No, I think you should . . . Yes, well all right. But it's your decision, just remember that. Don't say I bullied you into it.'

He threw a look at Jim, the kind that showed he hoped Jim had given up and gone. Then he rasped another few words into the receiver and ended the call. Irascible was the word. Reynoldes was irascible.

'Now then.' He advanced on Jim. 'What do you want?'

Jim's interest in meeting the man outweighed the knowledge that he'd chosen altogether the worst moment to do so and that he ought to retreat, not tackle Reynoldes about unanswered correspondence. He gave his name. This triggered no recognition. Jim explained that as his complaint through formal channels had been disregarded he'd come to . . .

Reynoldes was stupefied, then livid. He abandoned anything he'd ever absorbed about good manners or public relations. He bawled and he slammed the door. Jim rang the bell. Reynoldes ignored it. Jim left.

The auburn-haired girlfriend's name was Jennifer Blake. Jim learned that from a neighbour when he went to Twickenham one afternoon on a pretext. The eighty-year-old woman in the adjoining semi-detached cottage was happy to be interrupted, too easily taken in by a plausible young man with a pleasing personality and apparently harmless questions.

'*Mrs* Blake, although she's not married any longer.' And she added various titbits that Jim jotted down if they could conceivably be relevant to the survey he claimed he was doing for the local council. Thanking her he left, with a warning not to let strangers into her house. He doubted it was advice she would heed.

He invented inquiries from potential customers to the west of Acton and saw to it that Shaw sent him on those visits rather than anyone else. Sometimes Jim took the train out to Richmond in his own time. He didn't confront Reynoldes again but he kept an eye on him, noting the occasions when Reynoldes took his girlfriend for a drink or a meal before going home, or else went to the Twickenham cottage with her. They never noticed him, it was normal to see the same faces in the same area and he did nothing to attract attention.

One evening they'd entered a bar near the river and he was sitting outside, marvelling at the mess the crew of a launch were getting themselves into and waiting for the couple to come back out. Usually they stayed about fifteen minutes, long enough for one drink, but he had known them eat there. He made up his mind to give them another ten minutes before moving off.

'Hello, it's you.'

The voice was right next to him, startling, but the face was smiling. Cuddly Penny Reynoldes, clad in her tracksuit and bearing her tennis racket, had found him.

'Hi, Penny. How's the tennis?'

She giggled. 'I'm about to find out, I haven't played for days.'

'Couldn't you get a court?'

'I expect I could have done but I had exams. Ugh, I hate exams. I'll be glad when they're all over.'

She really was a nice kid, and he didn't want her to be there when her father and his mistress came out of the door ten feet away. He stood up. 'You going to the courts over that way?'

'Yes, we always play there. Except that sometimes I play with a friend whose family have got a simply huge garden with their own court.'

'I'll walk along with you,' he offered, leading the way and denying her the chance to say no.

They walked on, chatting about the things happening on the river, about her sports and about her hopes of college in the autumn.

'Actually,' she said, sounding like her mother as she did so, 'I had some information about a college course today but it's Mummy's evening for her interior-design class and Daddy's late again, so I haven't been able to discuss it with either of them yet.'

When they reached the courts she stopped a short way off to say goodbye. 'It's been so nice seeing you again, Jim. Thanks for the escort.' Then she ran to join her friends and answer their inevitable questions about him. He hadn't told her anything, not really. He never did tell people anything.

Penny went on court quite soon, a game of mixed doubles. That one, he assumed, was Clive, the one she said always partnered her. Jim saw the first few points. Penny and Clive won them easily. Penny had explained that she and Clive were becoming an effective team, that he was much better than she was. She hadn't said how highly Clive rated her game but Jim could see for himself that Clive admired Penny Reynoldes.

Clive looked around Penny's age, eighteen, and they made

34

an attractive couple, both fair and rounded. When they had to confer over tactics he would put a hand on her shoulder and when they changed ends he patted her head affectionately. Penny seemed to accept all this and Jim found himself wondering what else they shared apart from an enthusiasm for tennis.

Back at Acton he parked the office van in the yard and was about to go round to the front door to drop the keys through the letterbox when he heard a cough from inside the office. Unseen, he peeped in and got the back view of Eric Shaw, standing by the desk and flicking over the pages of an account book. Absorbed, Shaw seemed not to have heard the van.

He couldn't see why Shaw needed to be there at that time of evening. The man had control of the books throughout his working day and as he was notoriously fussy about details errors were unlikely. Puzzling over it, Jim caught the train home.

Geordie's voice reached him before he was through the front door in Tubbs Road. A couple of times a week Geordie had one or other of his drinking pals round to the ground-floor flat, and this was one of those times. If events followed the usual pattern, conviviality would end around ten o'clock with a shouting match or possibly a fist fight during which nobody was injured because nobody was sufficiently clear-headed to land a blow. During the jolly phase Geordie was capable of asking Jim to join them, a compliment Jim had learned to dodge.

Jim crept down the hall and upstairs. His door and window were wide open and Stefan was leaning on his sill. Jim choked back his annoyance.

'Guess I forgot to lock up,' he said mildly.

Stefan spared a glance over his shoulder. 'Hello, Jim. I came up to see if you were in but you weren't.'

Jim forbore to mention that most people would have reacted by going back to their own rooms, not entering his. He took off his good cotton jacket and hung it in the cupboard, automatically spacing the hangers along the rail.

Stefan was transfixed by a sleeper skimming through on

the northward run, some bogie flats gathering speed, a line of hoppers curving past a trundling Underground train. 'I reckon there's more of them. I mean, when I came here I'm sure there weren't as many trains as this.'

'Oh yes? You think they're breeding down at Euston, do you?'

'Eh?'

'I only . . . Oh, it doesn't matter. Coffee?' There was beer but he had an idea it wouldn't go down well with the drugs Stefan had been prescribed.

'Thanks.' Stefan tried and failed to stuff his shirt back into his waistband. In the sharp light of the window Jim noticed how deep-scored were the lines on Stefan's face. He couldn't help comparing the face with the healthily plump features of Penny's Clive. There was an age difference – twenty-three against eighteen – but it wasn't enough to account for the contrast. Clive had the face of a middle-class lad who knew that life would always be good to him, and Stefan had learned that for him it never would be.

Stefan's grubby-nailed hands were gripping the bottom of the window frame as, mesmerized by the trains, he hogged the view. 'They had a Pullman stopped out there for about ten minutes. Dodgy signal somewhere, I expect.'

Jim mumbled interest. He filled the kettle at the sink, and set the water tank grumbling behind the partition in the corner of his room and the pipes through the house banging. Once he'd plugged in the kettle he made Stefan make space for him at the window. The sky was sepia, unnatural. It tinged the rails reddish and stole the silvery sheen from metal swarf piled in the scrapyards. The great space beyond the junction was lost to a bleary haze, the hospital and the prison secreted away.

'Smog,' he said.

Stefan said: 'Eh?'

'Pollution making the sky that colour.'

Stefan was disbelieving. 'London doesn't have smog now. Anyway it was in the winter, not summertime.'

Jim let him win and switched off the kettle that ought to have done the job itself but was worn out. He spooned smog-brown powder into a couple of mugs. London didn't talk about its summer smogs, he'd discovered that rapidly enough. People didn't want to believe it so they pretended it wasn't happening. But every year since he'd come to the country he'd checked the sky on summer evenings and he'd recognized the tell-tale banding, the give-away brown, as car fumes and power stations pumped nitric acid, hydrogen peroxides, peroxyacetyl nitrates and aldehydes into the bright blue yonder. The human race delights in deception.

In Los Angeles, when he'd been bumming around California, smog was an unavoidable topic of conversation. The health hazards of it, the degree of it, the controls and their failures: everyone talked all the while about smog. He'd hit a bad season there, one of the city's worst, and it would have made sense to get out to the coast, move on, leave it all behind. Jim had been reluctant. He'd been high on the vitality of the town, drugged by the glamour. And there'd been the girl too.

Jim and the girl hadn't worked out, not entirely. He'd wasted a summer of his teens hoping it would come right and when it was plain it was never going to do that, then he'd made for the coast. Those long, long beaches and the surf swinging in. He'd got a board, idled a month or two hanging out in the beach places doing what folks did when they were doing nothing much at all. And then he'd grown restless. Always he grew restless.

'Jim?'

Stefan had spoken to him but he hadn't heard. He raised an inquiring eyebrow. Stefan repeated. 'I said that man came for you today. You know, the one who came before I was ill.'

A muscle tightened in Jim's stomach. 'The guy that drives the old car with the blue metallic paint?'

Stefan was impressed with this precision of memory. 'Yes that's right.'

'And what did he want?'

'Dunno. He spoke to Geordie. I saw him go away, that's all.' Stefan lifted his mug and gulped coffee before saying that it wasn't sweet enough.

Jim pushed the jar with the sugar and the encrusted spoon across the Formica table towards him.

After the coffee was drunk he eased Stefan out and went downstairs to question Geordie. Geordie was rheumy eyed, on the verge of changing from an affable drunk to an antagonistic one. Jim kept the interview short, staying in the doorway rather than join Geordie's other visitor in the fug of the flat. He was given a description: medium height, brown hair and an accent that Geordie said was Irish. Jim recalled Stefan saying it was Scottish. No matter, it was safe to assume it was the same man because it was the same car. The caller hadn't told Geordie what he wanted. Jim was moving away when a comment was flung after him.

'But I can tell you this, he had the shoes. They think you can't tell but you always can.'

Jim dismissed this with an incredulous laugh, and ran up the first flight of stairs. Geordie leaned out into the passage and shouted: 'You take my word, he's the police for sure.'

Round the bend, out of Geordie's sight, Jim's face changed. He didn't doubt the old man's instinct. A policeman on the doorstep was among his deepest fears. Any day he'd be off on his new track and he needed a smooth run. A delicate time for the police to come pestering.

He burst into his room, torn between the desire to flee and the need for calm. One moment he was scrabbling the folder of newspaper cuttings out of its hiding place and wrapping it in a bag, the next he was unwrapping it and putting it back. He stood, clenching his fists, thinking, *thinking*. Then he pulled a jacket from the wardrobe, slipped one arm into a sleeve before taking the garment off.

'*Shit!*'

He dropped on to the bed, his arm catching the lamp with the forget-me-not shade and dislodging it. He writhed, clutched at the falling china and saved it. From below came the buzz of Stefan's television. Two floors below Geordie and his friend were arguing. Outside the trains swooped by. But the soothing monotony of life in Tubbs Road had changed.

Sighing, he went to the window and drew the sash down. Carriages were lighted, they flung streaks of orange over adjacent lines, this way and that, straight as an arrow, or wandering along local lines, strangely high up on the ramp of the North London line . . . Always the trains.

Expresses went through too fast for infantile chanting. *Wzzzzzzzzzzzzzz*, and they were receding specks of yellow glow. The slower ones let in the words. *'Time to move, time to move, time to move.'*

Jim stepped away from the window, his back to the trains' insistence and the ugliness that had been his company for months. He wished he could vanish as abruptly as one of those expresses unleashed at Euston.

He counted money, not cash but bank money. Enough. Not princely but adequate to begin. Once he'd begun there'd be no problem about where the rest was coming from. He reached on top of the wardrobe for his bag. With care he placed his possessions in it. A few clothes. The folder of cuttings and some paperback novels. He straightened, shook his head. This was wrong. If nothing else, he should take the precaution of a telephone call.

Leaving the bag on his bed, locking up, he hurried to a payphone in a pub corridor. Around 10.00 p.m. London time, and afternoon in New York. Not a bad time to talk. Daubeney took the call himself. It sounded as though he had a mouthful of sandwich but anyway he said what Jim hoped to hear. 'Sure I can tell you that.'

'Go right ahead.'

Jim listened as he ran through it. 'A date,' said Jim finally. 'Can you give me a date?'

'The twelfth.'

'You're sure of that?'

'I swear.'

'Great. And thanks.'

'Hey, just one thing before you hang up, Jim. I wish you luck with whatever it is, but I don't ever want to know about it, OK?'

'OK.'

The twelfth. Not so very long. Too long, though, to be skipping from Tubbs Road tonight. He made a So-what? face

39

and went into the bar and drank a secret toast to the twelfth, the day his life would change.

He tied up loose ends. He shopped for a suit, a good one, with an Italian label. There were other smaller purchases to be made and for these he didn't risk a second trip to central London but took the train to Richmond. Perhaps he knew all along that he was going to look up Penny Reynoldes.

She'd never suggested she played tennis on Saturday afternoons but he wished it was so and he found her at the courts. Penny, flushed with a mixture of exertion and triumph, defeated a girl with a wicked backhand.

'Voyeurism,' she accused, running across. 'You'll get a bad reputation if you hang around the courts while young ladies are at play.'

'Then we'll go for a coffee.'

Her hesitation was momentary, then she agreed. The hesitation was explained as Clive appeared, asking: 'Penny, are you nearly ready?' He looked from her to Jim, his jaw tightening, bringing a firmer look to the rounded features. Penny introduced them, first names, nothing more. Jim said hello and Clive nodded. Clive spoke to Penny again. 'Well?' Already he sounded defeated.

Most of the group by the court watched the encounter, but when Clive walked back to them alone they were all busy cramming clothes into hold-alls, testing racket strings, tying shoelaces.

Penny changed into a T-shirt and skirt no longer than her tennis dress, and then led Jim to a café and a table overlooking the river. She told him about the art deco interior and the building's origins as a ballroom, but Jim was in no doubt that she'd taken him there to show him off to her friends rather than to show him an aspect of Richmond.

Being flaunted didn't displease him. When it came time to leave, Penny said goodbye to the faces she knew and Jim smiled at them. Penny's friends had a similarity. Jim assumed they all lived in houses like the Reynoldeses', or older variations of it, that they'd enjoyed identical upbringings and would proceed to lead comparably comfortable lives. He found it as easy to generalize about them as about the West Indians of Willesden.

They were in the street. Penny asked where his car was.

'Oh . . . er . . . I didn't bring it.'

'I was going to cadge a lift home, but maybe it's better that I don't. If I arrive with you instead of Clive, there'll be comments. I'll get a lift from Sarah, one of the girls in the café. She'll be driving up that way shortly.'

'No problem if you arrive with Sarah?'

'Exactly.'

She fixed her lift and he left her at the café. He didn't want to go. He wanted to spend the rest of the day with her, but couldn't. He wished he'd made a date to meet her again, but hadn't. Leaving her, he felt lonely.

Jim walked over the bridge to the Twickenham side, moving briskly but without an end in sight. He took the riverside path south, past playing fields and a street or two, and then the open land of Marble Hill. A wind was getting up, clouds thrusting in from the west and flotsam racing downriver. Trees overhanging the path began to sway. The brightness of the day was blown away.

He cut inland, along a footpath, seeking shelter from the rain he anticipated. He hoped for a bus to Richmond station, a train home. This was no longer an evening for lonesome walks. But when he reached a main road he realized he was close to the street where Jennifer Blake lived. He was tempted to see whether Matthew Reynoldes's car was there.

A block of yellow light fell across the pavement from the uncurtained bay window. Jennifer was kneeling in front of the fireplace, her auburn hair loose and screening her face from him. He saw her put a match to the wood. The room was prepared for a visitor. Two glasses and an unopened bottle of red wine stood on a table near the fireplace. Jennifer rose, stepped back and looked down into the fire, willing it to catch. A rush of flame and she moved away, brushing dust from her hands, and went through a door on the far side of the room.

Jim crossed the road, to see more closely. There was a dining table, laid for two and decorated with freesias in a thin porcelain vase. Her table linen was pink and white, picking up the colours in the pattern on her china. The glassware was etched with a delicate pattern. The room was feminine and pretty, it wasn't furnished cheaply nor skimped in any way. Jim wondered how much of it Matthew Reynoldes had paid for.

Reynoldes was presumably due that evening, all that Jennifer Blake had left to do was to change out of her jeans. The clothes Jim had previously seen her in were strictly office wear, good linen suits and smart dresses that showed she had a serious job. In jeans and with her hair down she looked younger. Not as young as Penny Reynoldes, but easily young enough to be Matthew Reynoldes's daughter.

She wasn't physically like Penny at all, she was spiky, slim to the point of thinness, and she had long-lashed brown eyes. Jim imagined her elegant in long black velvet, the kind of outfit that would make a girl of Penny's build podgy. But long black velvet wouldn't be worn for a tête-à-tête supper at home, so he cast around for another image of Jennifer entertaining her lover.

The first drops of rain interrupted him and he walked on, troubled by questions. Minutes later people were fleeing through the streets, dogs were having their walks cut short, children were abandoning playing fields, and gardeners were gathering up tools and scurrying inside. The shower was a downpour. Jim dived into a pub, shook water from his hair and ordered a Scotch. After that he ordered another.

He couldn't get Matthew Reynoldes out of his head. Reynoldes's job, his house, his wife, his daughter, his mistress. Jim knew a lot about Matthew Reynoldes but none of it assuaged his need to know more. Sometimes he got like that about people. When he was a boy he'd clipped a newspaper for stories about Clyde Rogan, a rock star. Other times he'd asked around, if the subjects weren't the sort to concern journalists, and he'd found out the places they went to and contrived to meet them.

He'd never met Clyde Rogan, he'd had to make do with Rusty Blair, a local boy who looked a lot like him. Jim could never meet Rusty without suffering a delicious confusion of fact and fantasy. Most of him realized that Rusty was only Rusty, but the other part thrilled to be near him. He first met him at the Weedons' place. It was one of those days when the wind breathed winter. An oyster sky lay over a drab hill, an old woman was tugged about as she beat a mat on her step, chimney smoke was diving and whirling, mad for escape, and Rusty stopped by to fetch eggs for his mother. They weren't ready.

Jim and Al Weedon sloped after him into the barn while the hens' secret places were exposed, their nests robbed. Rusty ignored the boys and talked to Al's mother, about Chicago and the things he'd seen there that she'd never believe. The boys hung around the track until his convertible was out of sight.

'We could do all that,' said Al, hands anchoring his hair. 'Go to Chicago, get a job and a car.'

'Sure.' But Jim didn't want what Rusty had, Clyde Rogan wasn't tied down to shift work on the line in a factory. Jim believed that one day when he had sufficient details he'd be able to pinpoint the magical difference between the people who led ordinary, uneventful lives and the lucky ones, like Clyde. His instinct was that the answer would turn out to be daring. Rusty Blair had chanced no more than moving over the state line to a routine job, while Clyde's life was an adventure story.

Penny Reynoldes had jokingly accused Jim of voyeurism, but she was wrong. It wasn't a need to look, it was a need to know. Another woman had referred to compulsion but, as he remembered, she'd been talking about risk-taking.

Once the rain slackened he returned to the street where Jennifer Blake lived and he rang her doorbell. Her curtains were drawn, there was no sign of Reynoldes's car. Jim asked after her neighbour, the old woman who had one day answered his questions about Jennifer.

'Did you hear her earlier today?' He was claiming he could get no answer at the house.

Jennifer frowned. 'Yes, I saw her just to say hello to this afternoon. I hope she's all right.'

She'd left her hair loose but caught it up at one side with

a silver slide. A creamy yellow dress draped her body, flattering her angularity. Jim had seen what he'd come for and was ready to go. In the room off the tiny entrance hall he heard a chair scrape. A man's voice called out: 'What is it, Jenny?'

The man appeared at her shoulder. He was dark, no more than thirty years old and he was a total stranger. Jim said he'd try the next house again and sloped off.

Had Reynoldes and Jennifer Blake split up? Or was the dark young man a secret from Reynoldes? Jim hoped it was a secret, he liked the thought of the duplicitous Reynoldes being tricked in the same way he was tricking his own wife. An incident the following week encouraged him to believe it. He was in the car park when the red car drove in and Jennifer kissed Reynoldes goodbye, hopped out and started up her blue hatchback.

Jim didn't follow either of them. He went to a callbox and rang Penny. 'A drink at the Dolphin?' he asked. That was a wine bar she'd told him she liked. 'I can pick you up in five minutes.'

'Park by the trees, down Queens Road a bit.'

'OK.'

He was relieved she'd suggested that. The last thing he fancied was meeting either of her parents again.

He pulled up near the trees and counted off the minutes until she came out of the courtyard. When her step faltered because she couldn't see a car he got out of the van and waved to her. Penny ran up, laughing. 'What on earth is this thing?'

'An office van. The door's open.'

She walked past the door and read the writing along the side. 'J. and J. Electrical'. He'd told her he owned his own business. She said: 'Is one of those Js for Jim, and if so who's the other J?'

'No, I told you I bought a business when I came over here. That's the name it already had.'

'Yes, but . . .'

'Come on, are we going to the Dolphin or are we going to

stand here discussing the writing on the van?' He got in so that if she was to continue talking she had to do so too.

Penny climbed in, looked into the back, then looked all around. 'Do you know, I don't think I've ever been in a van before.'

He wasn't surprised, but he wished she wouldn't go on about it. He tried to get her to talk about something else, *anything* else. Unfortunately the van was a trigger for a string of inquiries about his business.

'No,' he said, with a degree of scorn. 'Of course I don't often drive this. But my car's being serviced and what's the point of having a fleet of vans if you don't make use of them in emergencies?'

'How many's a fleet, in this instance?'

'Five.' He narrowly avoided adding that it was one for each shop as he realized claiming to own five shops would be excessive.

'Who normally drives this one?'

'Eric, one of my shop managers. But he's off sick so he won't be needing it.' He made a left turn.

Penny shrieked. 'No! It was straight on there.' After that hiccup she concentrated on directing him and dropped the questions. But he could virtually hear her mind cashing up what his business was worth. Penny often talked about money, not necessarily directly but she had a calculator brain, aware how much everything cost and which were the expensive nice things to aspire to.

Clive's parents had given him a sports car for his eighteenth birthday, which wasn't uncommon in her circle. And his parents owned a cottage in the Cotswolds where they went most weekends leaving him and his brother to fend for themselves. Her friend Sarah had been bought some fantastic designer clothes and was being taken to New York for a month to meet family friends who moved in the smartest circles. Snippets like these peppered Penny's conversation, creating an unambiguous picture of the world she inhabited.

Jim, in turn, assessed what the Reynoldeses were worth, and it was substantially more than Matthew Reynoldes's salary. Penny had revealed that her mother's parents had left them money that had partly paid for the building of the house in Queens Road. Besides that house there was a modest lochside boat-house in Scotland. Also, her mother wasn't attending those classes in interior design but was giving them. She was a partner in one of the many businesses of that type in Richmond.

Penny joked about the van again when Jim drove her home. 'Just let me out at the roundabout, Jim. Mummy would die if she saw me getting out of a van.'

He joked about it too, playing the role he'd written for himself, the boss borrowing one of the fleet vehicles in a crisis. The smiling stopped immediately she left him. The van had been a miscalculation. He'd never use it again, she wasn't the type of girl prepared to be seen around the place in a van. Once was a novelty, but once was enough.

Hurt by her attitude, he was in no hurry to see her again and he avoided Richmond altogether. It was Eric Shaw who sent him back there, to advise the owner of a block of twenty flats about installing a satellite dish on the flat roof.

Jim objected: '*Richmond*, Eric? Why would a guy who lives right over there want to talk to us?'

Shaw's eyes narrowed but when he replied the remark was no more cutting than: 'Don't mock the customer who wishes to give us his business.'

Alex was there too. 'Jim's right, it doesn't make sense, Eric. There must be somebody nearer who could do it for him.'

Shaw wore a sour half-smile as he said: 'Perhaps our reputation has gone before us.'

He passed Jim a sheet with details: Mr Norton at Maple Court, off Petersham Road. Then Jim read the final line: 8.30 p.m. So that explained Shaw's relative good humour, he was able to tie up Jim's evening. Jim stuffed the paper in his jacket pocket.

Norton was late and the caretaker didn't know he was due there. Jim sat in the van, listening to the radio and checking each vehicle that drew into the leafy parking area. He let half an hour pass and then he paced around. The caretaker offered him a telephone number to call Norton. Norton's telephone wasn't answered.

Jim asked to be allowed up on the roof to carry out his survey, but the man grew less obliging. He had instructions not to give access to unauthorized people and for all he knew Jim had no genuine authority. Better wait for Mr Norton.

Jim sat in the van again. Eventually he left a message that he was going to get something to eat and asked that if Norton arrived he should wait until Jim returned.

As parking in the town was difficult, he went on foot. Shaw, he supposed, had made a mistake in writing down the details, muddled the day perhaps. He walked on, looking out over the river and the long views beyond it, at trees and green spaces, his thoughts carrying him far away. Without warning a car going up Richmond Hill swerved across the road, braked, and the driver shouted. 'You there, I want to talk to you.'

Matthew Reynoldes. Jim glanced round. There was no one else close enough to be the target. Reynoldes said: 'Yes, *you*. I want to know what you think you're up to.'

Vehicles were swinging downhill, round the obstruction of Reynoldes's car. The drivers had a clear view of the confrontation. Jim forced a smile, trying to give those drivers a false impression of the encounter.

'Hello, Mr Reynoldes.'

'Now look here,' said Reynoldes. 'You've got some explaining to do.'

Jim held the smile intact. 'But surely I've been waiting for *your* explanation, Mr Reynoldes. Waiting quite some time, in fact.'

A passing car hooted, having trouble getting past as traffic was now speeding uphill as well as down. 'I've got to move,' said Reynoldes. 'Get in.'

'What?'

'In. Just get in.'

Jim opened the rear door because it was safer than stepping out into the traffic. He wriggled across to the far side, noting the lush springiness of the upholstery, the real wood trim. Then he concentrated on Reynoldes's face, the aspect of it

47

he could see from that angle. There were prominent veins in the neck, a muscle twitching at the corner of the mouth.

Reynoldes said nothing and drove fast, so fast that at the complicated roundabout junction at the top he cut in front of another driver who had the right of way. Jim clenched, pressed back into the corner of the seat and waited for the impact. Reynoldes braked and slewed. The other car went on its way. After that they went more carefully but the ride was jerky with Jim's head brushing the suede lining of the roof. By the time Reynoldes stopped, he felt sick.

They stood on opposite sides of the car. Jim had never been so far into the park before. Reynoldes marched towards a stand of oakwood, motioning Jim to follow. Away from the road, masked from it by trees, Reynoldes faced him. They were roughly the same height, Reynoldes heavier. His colour was up and his eyes burned with a rage he didn't care to suppress. When he spoke his chin jutted.

'I don't know what kind of nut you are, but I want you out of my life. I don't want you near my house and I don't want you near my daughter ever again. Have you got that?'

Jim stayed calm. 'I haven't harmed you, Mr Reynoldes. I'm owed an apology by you, you've kept me waiting for it.'

Reynoldes got a grip on the front of Jim's good jacket. The fabric twisted, dragging against Jim's neck. The face drew closer, not the likeable face of the posters but the private face, the one warped with bitterness. 'Damn your fucking apology. You think you can harangue me on my own doorstep, sniff around my daughter . . . God, you've got a nerve. I ought to report you to the police.'

Jim pushed at the hand clutching his jacket but Reynoldes held firm. Jim said: 'You'd look pretty foolish doing that, a father complaining to the police because he doesn't like his daughter's choice of company.'

That's when Reynoldes brought up his other fist and hit him. Jim heard the sharp intake of his own breath, broke the grip on his jacket, regained his balance and attempted to duck the ensuing blow. He didn't want to have to hit the older man. He said so, but a third blow landed and he couldn't dodge away from it because he'd backed up against a tree. He closed with Reynoldes.

They struggled, neither of them having room to get in a swing. Then Jim worked a foot behind an ankle and jerked Reynoldes off-balance in an attempt to throw him down. Reynoldes staggered but clung. And Jim heard a soft tearing sound as the material of his jacket parted under the strain. The damage spurred his anger as much as anything that had happened. He fell on to Reynoldes, forcing him down, rolling with him, wishing he could smash his skull on the ground.

Reynoldes was groaning, too winded for cursing but holding on. Jim felt disgusted, at Reynoldes and at himself. He slackened his grip, wrenched out of the man's grasp and moved back on hands and knees, catching his breath. After a few seconds he tilted his head for a sideways look at Reynoldes. The man was snuffling but immobile, his eyes were shut.

Jim stood up and inspected the damage. His jacket sleeve was half-out, there were grubby marks down his trousers and his shoes were scuffed. He expected a black eye and his left forearm was sore. He rubbed it. Then he looked at Reynoldes again. The man hadn't made any effort to rise.

Moving swiftly, Jim squatted beside him, loosened Reynoldes's tie and undid the top buttons of his shirt. He rolled back an eyelid. Reynoldes was unconscious. Jim straightened and looked around. Nobody was in sight, although there were the lights of intermittent cars on the road through the park. It was near dusk, light was fading as he figured out what to do.

Reynoldes needed a doctor. No, a hospital. Jim felt in the man's pockets for his car keys. He thought about carrying him, but it was too far and it would be more efficient to fetch the car over the grass. He started running away from the trees, then cut his speed as a car coursed the road. He didn't want to draw attention.

Reynoldes had parked the car in gear and it leaped forward as Jim started the engine. He stalled, restarted and moved gingerly towards the trees.

Jim manoeuvred him into the back seat, head down on the

soft leather. Then he inched the car towards the road. He was trying to remember where there was a hospital, and also what was likely to happen when he took Reynoldes in there. Details, of course. There was certain to be someone whose task it was to write down who Jim and Reynoldes were and what had occurred. Jim shied away from that. He thought of disappearing once he'd handed the patient to the casualty team.

Richmond Gate was getting near, he had to reach a decision. And he was increasingly reluctant to go to the hospital. No amount of charm would soothe the staff into believing that he wasn't responsible for Reynoldes's condition, his own battered state would point to it.

Jim stopped the car just inside the gate and leaned over into the back seat. Reynoldes was absolutely still. Jim felt for a pulse. He didn't find one. A park keeper was waiting to lock the gates for the night and waved him through. Before he knew he'd settled anything, Jim was driving down Star and Garter Hill, away from the town and medical help. He joined Petersham Road, entered River Lane, cut the car lights and rolled forward.

Ahead there was nothing but the Thames, a sign warning drivers not to get too close. A dangerous place, it flooded there. There were no lamps, no houses, no pubs. In the darkness it was desolate. Jim welcomed the darkness.

First he ripped out the car radio, tore the tax disc off the windscreen, rifled the glove box and side pockets for odds and ends. Some he put with the radio into a plastic carrier bag taken from one of the shelves, the rest he scattered in the front passenger well. Throughout, he wore Reynoldes's driving gloves. Then he dragged the man from the rear and repositioned him in the driving seat, anxiety making nothing of the weight. Finally he used a handful of tissues from a box beneath the dashboard to rub over every surface inside the car and also the exterior handles, anything he knew he'd touched and many things he knew he hadn't. Jim left the car unlocked, the front windows wound down and the key in the ignition. He walked to the river, the plastic bag swinging in his hand.

There was a towpath. A good way along it to the west, he sat in the cover of riverbank trees and waited for the darkness to deepen. He thought about the fight, trying to recall whether he'd succeeded in crashing Reynoldes's head on the ground or whether the man's struggles had prevented the contact. He was almost sure he'd failed and Reynoldes had won. Absurd, to be considering it in terms of failure and victory.

Jim shuddered and drew his torn jacket around him. He shut out memories of the fight and grew practical, transferring a small torch from the plastic bag to his pocket. There was a curve of moon, that was all. The time would arrive, fairly soon, when he would need a torch. Walking along the towpath had been no whim, he had a vague plan and he needed to think it through while the pressure was off. Later he might be forced to make rapid decisions and he meant to be prepared for them.

Fingers explored his aching eye. Reynoldes was right-handed. When his fist had thudded into Jim's face, he'd used the left fist because the other was clutching the jacket. The blow had been true, though. Jim felt the puffiness, the eye starting to close, and the pain, inevitably the pain. He winced, drew his hand away, bit a lip.

By contrast, Reynoldes had looked unscathed. Jim hadn't aimed a single blow at his face. In truth, almost all his moves had been defensive. He shook his head, bewildered. He'd controlled himself when many men mightn't have and what good had it achieved? Reynoldes was dead just as surely as if Jim had laid into him with all the force of his twenty-five years.

A rat ran along the bank ahead of him. He flicked the torch at it and it skittered away. He shone the beam on his watch, but the glass was cracked and it had stopped. Time to move, anyway.

A few hundred yards further west he saw the dark shadow he was relying on. With stealth he approached. No sound but the suck of water on the bank, no lights but the sliver of moon. The slope of the bank was steep, there was mud. He skidded, snatched at the thin branch of a sapling, saved himself. Creatures whispered in the undergrowth. A piece of driftwood clunked against timber and then spun away into mid-stream.

Jim drew a deep breath and edged forward, stepping over ropes, getting a foot on a gangplank, bouncing it to test for safety, trusting it and gliding up on the deck of the boat. The tide was high, she was swaying, a modest old cruiser hidden in the blackness. He peered, more or less felt his way to her stern, dodged ropes and paraphernalia, risked a flicker of torchlight over the side, was reassured by what he saw, and dared to lower himself down over the slavering waters.

His foot made contact with a hard rim, he shifted and tried again. Down, tentatively, then rapidly as his hand slipped on the rail. An arm wrenched and he committed himself. As he landed the tender bucked and he grabbed at it, anyhow, trapping his hand as she recoiled against the hull of the cruiser. A thin cry of pain escaped him. He slumped, dead centre, his weight balancing and steadying the tender and he pressed the injured hand against his body and fought down the pain. Then he freed the bag that hung from his other wrist and lay it down in front of him.

There was no paddle to hand. He'd assumed it would be in the tender and he was forced to try and climb back up to search the cruiser for it. Ascent was no easier, but he made it and came upon a pair of oars on the deck. Within seconds he had dropped down again and was freeing the ropes that secured the tender, letting her ride the tide.

The tide wanted to take her along by the bank where trees hung low over the water. He was trying to fix the oars in rowlocks, take control of her, but he was fumbling, unable to see what he was doing, aware chiefly of the trees looming ahead and the creamy froth where waves smacked into them. The strength of the current worried him.

Jim abandoned one of the oars in the bottom of the tender and used the other to fend off as she was swirled and about to go broadside into heavy driftwood caught against the bowing trees. He shoved her away, clear but not far enough for safety. The effort allowed him seconds to set up the rhythm of the oars, ignoring rowlocks and working desperately, drawing out into midstream, fighting the tug of the tide.

The river was sounds and secrets. As clouds passed the arc of the moon the Thames was reduced to a heavy, hissing mass hidden from his sight. No reflection, no sense of where he'd been or where he was heading, only movement and a cool breath of air on his sweating skin. He chose one of those sightless passages to drift, emptying the plastic bag upside down over the side and relinquishing the radio, the driving gloves and all the other items from the car. The bag itself he pushed into his pocket. Taking up the oars again he fought his way towards the Twickenham side. The current was dragging him back. Every inch he won was exhausting.

Something collided with him, something longer than the tender and hellbent on forcing him downriver. He floundered, attempted to run ahead of it and found it kept pace, pushing, goading him in the direction he was determined not to go. Cloud freed the moon, his eyes focused on the long stout branch of a big tree, its finer branches and leaves rearing up at one end. He jabbed at it with an oar, praying for it to whirl by and leave him alone. He gained a couple of feet along its length and then became ensnared in its twigs and sprigs. The tender bobbed among them. Part of the branch was submerged and Jim sensed the scraping wood beneath the boat, the threat to upset him.

He stabbed again and again, the tender tilted, water slapped over the rim. Still the branch had him snared. He dropped both oars by his feet, got a hand among the twigs. The twigs scratched his face. He sank back, it was futile. Taking up the oars again he rowed with frantic energy, ahead of the treacherous tree top but away at an angle.

There was a bend in the river, and it was coming up very fast. If he didn't escape before then the tender would be wrecked. His eye was closing, he had little vision on his right side. His arm was sore where Reynoldes had hit him and the hand that had been squeezed between the tender and the cruiser was throbbing. He gritted his teeth and kept the desperate pace of his rowing.

Several times he skimmed away from the branch but the

curve of the river encouraged it to chase and catch him, pushing him broadside. Twice there was adequate light for him to see the shape of a finer branch of the same piece of tree lifting up from the water ahead of his prow, lifting and then dropping down, appearing briefly and then again as a reminder just when he risked hoping he might escape.

His teeth savaged his lower lip. Everything ached: the muscles that kept the oars in action, the injuries, and his head from the tension and the fear. He was on the verge of panic.

All of a sudden the solid end of the branch clipped another obstacle, the tangled end shot up, raising the tender and flinging it round towards mid-stream. Jim's oars flailed air. The full extent of the finer branch was exposed for a couple of seconds, then it fell and as it went the tender slapped down. He registered the speed, the water flooding over his feet, an oar torn from his left hand. And then the snarl of twigs that had toyed with him for so long closed over his head.

The torch was gone. That's what he thought. Simply that the torch was gone. The tender was gone too, he was snagged among the hurtling mass of vegetation and he could no longer feel the tender below him. He was facing the Richmond bank but right out in mid-river without a chance of reaching land. Swimming was impossible, he couldn't move quickly enough and the branch would ride over him, drown him. He spat out water, heaved himself through the ripping, tearing tree and tried to reach a position where he could ride the solid trunk.

He slipped. He felt his flesh was shredded and his clothes worse, but he managed to do it. And as he hung, panting, over the broad black wet bark he opened his good eye and was amazed to see the tender, close by, caught in the wake. The sight spurred him on. He drew himself up on to the branch. Crouching, he edged along it until he was lined up with the tender, its prow a little to his left to minimize the danger of being run down by it.

Jim threw himself into the water. His right hand fastened on the rim, he brought his left round to join it and willpower carried him over the edge. It was wet in there, extremely, but he was afloat and there was one oar. He paddled away from the wake, loosing the leafy strands that towed the tender, and he settled for the Richmond side of the river until the branch was well clear. Then he paddled across, let the current throw him ashore anywhere it chose on the Twickenham side. When the prow aimed for a dark patch where flotsam from higher tides was trapped in a tree, and debris bobbed in the makeshift anchorage between natural vegetation and dumped rubbish, he didn't argue with it. Jim hauled himself ashore.

His last act before turning inland was to shove the tender off to rejoin the current.

Three

Trains scything darkness, the wind trailing misery. Jim rubbed a steamy patch on his window pane. Reynoldes was dead . . . Or was he? Perhaps he hadn't been when he was dumped at the riverside. Perhaps he'd died later because of the panicky decision not to head for the hospital. Supposing . . .

Breath misted the pane again. Below another train howled. Often they signalled hope, those trains, with their eager energy and their destinations, their rhythmic progress. *On our way, on our way, on our way* . . . But times like this night, when a grudging moon failed to raise a glint from the steel of rail and scrap, these times there were no words to fit their sound, nothing but an answering moan from a mind in pain.

The right eye was closed, his face and body lacerated, his shoes and clothes sodden and ruined. He'd limped to the van that way, skulking in darkened streets, avoiding passers-by and driving to Willesden. He'd gone straight to the mirror, appalled. He minded about the clothes, but more that his good looks were marred. If it had been possible, he'd have hidden in his room until his face healed.

Vanity was a sin he acknowledged. Never could he be like Stefan with his jumble-sale clothes, his badly cut hair and his reluctance to wash. Nor could he drink himself into premature old age like Geordie of the pouched face and greyish hue. He demanded better and he knew how to get it. He'd done it before and he could do it again.

His thoughts ran to those carefree California days, riding the surf, making a little here and a little there, just enough to keep going until the big chance came. And when it didn't, going right out to fetch it. When people asked him where he came from he often said California. He might equally well have said New York or Boston because he'd lived there too. Repetition was seductive. Some of the lies he was beginning to believe himself.

Yet when he lay on the ragged bedcover and listened to the trains going through the junction their sound hooked a memory of other trains, high American trains towering through neat towns in the hawkeye state. And trains cutting a countryside of white clapboard houses, silver silos, golden corn and black suspicion. That famous image of the old couple with the pitchfork, that could stand for his grandparents, or so he was inclined to believe. But not to say. California, is what he told people instead.

Rain tickled the window pane. Daylight streaked the sky. Jim lay awake, awaiting the new day and a lessening of pain and anxiety, but also an apologetic telephone call to Eric Shaw.

'I can't make it today, I have the flu,' he said. 'Oh and . . . er . . . I have the van also. I used it to get home last night. That job at the flats in Richmond, your Mr Norton didn't show.'

Shaw was caustic, making out that the loss of the van for the day was a major catastrophe in the history of J. and J. Jim hunched over the phone in the public callbox and let the criticism fly by. When Shaw paused he said: 'Maybe I'll get it over to you later today.' He hung up.

Back in Tubbs Road he found Stefan using his room for train spotting. Aching, irritated, Jim objected to him wandering in and out as he chose. He had never understood why Stefan was hesitant when he was there but paradoxically had no compunction about marching in when he wasn't.

Stefan didn't appreciate the paradox let alone attempt to explain it. He was cowed. He offered to go.

Jim, already regretting his harshness, continued to snap. 'Oh for heaven's sake, do what you like.'

Stefan gaped. 'Jim, your face! What happened?'

'Nothing. It's no big deal.'

'You look awful. That eye's going to be really . . .'

'Yes, sure. Look, if you're staying do you want a coffee?' He bent over the mugs and things on the table, concealing his face from Stefan's childlike scrutiny.

'Thanks,' said Stefan. 'You staying home from work because of that?'

'The flu, that's what I told them.'

'Well they wouldn't want to send you out looking like that, would they?'

Terse, Jim agreed. He didn't like Stefan going on about the way he looked.

Stefan said: 'It'll take a few days, that eye.'

Jim tossed coffee powder into the mugs. 'I thought you'd come up here to watch the trains.'

'Eh?'

'Oh forget it.' He gave in. His injuries were the best excitement in Stefan's life for weeks. Jim hovered near the kettle, poised to switch it off. If he wasn't quick it steamed the wallpaper off.

Stefan was manageable, Geordie less so. Jim poured, stirred in a creamy powder and added sugar with extra for Stefan. Jim said: 'Would you mind not saying anything to Geordie? If he wants to know anything, just say I have the flu. OK?'

'All right.' Stefan pointed to a bundle, tied in a plastic bag, inside the door. 'You want me to take any rubbish down to the dustbin for you? I mean, it would stop you running into Geordie.'

'Thanks.' There wasn't much to go, a bag of bits and pieces from a pedal bin plus the bag Stefan had noticed. That one contained the damaged clothes and shoes. When Stefan left, nearly an hour later, he took both bags away with him. Jim lay down and fell asleep.

He woke to a heavy tread on the top flight of stairs. All the fears of the past night distilled in those unfamiliar footsteps. Tense, he forced himself to lie there, give some semblance of being relaxed. The pain in his head resumed, passing from the damaged eye and up over his skull to meet the knot of pain in the muscles of his neck and shoulders.

'The door's open,' he said when the knock came. His voice was satisfactorily drowsy.

The door creaked. Jim didn't move. He blinked up, then frowned. 'What do you want?'

The man was thirtyish, hair receding at the temples, clothes casual but a year or two out of date and showing signs of wear. Like Geordie had said, it was the shoes that gave it away.

'You're Jim Rush?' A dull south London accent.

Jim sat up, not bothering to conceal the pain in every movement, exaggerating it possibly. 'Who are you?' The name was immaterial. The police had come, that was what mattered.

An identification card flickered and was withdrawn. 'Detective Sergeant Boulter.'

Jim swung his feet over the side of the bed. 'That chair's more or less comfortable if you'd care to sit down.'

Boulter went to the chair but didn't sit. He looked out on to the tracks instead. Then he leaned with his back to the window and took a critical look at Jim. 'Christ,' he said, but there was no sympathy. 'What does the other guy look like this morning?'

'Which one of them?'

A grin spread over the policeman's face. 'Upset a whole bunch of people, did you?'

'Just two. Or maybe it was three. A bit of a blur, if you want to know.'

'Looks like you've been drinking in the wrong pub.'

Jim sighed, ran fingers over his puffy eye. 'Look, could we talk about what you came for?'

'Get off the painful subject, eh?' He laughed at his pathetic joke.

Jim didn't.

Boulter said: 'I've got some dates I want to put to you.' He recited three. 'Well then, where were you?'

'They were weekdays?'

'A Tuesday and two Thursdays.'

'Then I was working.'

'Still at J. and J. Electrical in Acton?'

59

'You know it, you just squeezed by the van to reach the front door.'

Then they went into times of day, on the Tuesday and two Thursdays. Jim ran a tentative hand along his sore forearm. 'Mind if I make some coffee while I think about this?'

He refilled the kettle, washed the mugs, talked above the sound of the water tank in the corner and said that it was impossible for him to give the answers offhand but the information was certain to be on the job list in the office.

'Eric Shaw, the deputy manager, he calls it a job list but it's a desk diary really. He writes down the jobs as they come in, puts initials against them. It'll be the only record I have, but . . .' He paused, a spoon in one hand and the coffee jar in the other. 'Well, I guess you won't be doing me any favours if you ask for it.'

Boulter raised an ironic eyebrow. 'Reckon you're owed a favour, do you, Jim?'

Jim shrugged. 'It's a job, isn't it?'

'And you love it and you don't want to lose it.' Sarcastic but not as sarcastic as Eric Shaw would be after an inquiry from the police.

'No,' said Jim equably. 'Shaw can be a bastard, he winds everybody up and he suffers from flights of fancy. But it's a job.'

He put a mug of coffee on the edge of the table. Boulter took it up immediately and began to drink in great gulps. An engine whipping across the junction screamed and he jolted round. 'Bloody hell. Do they keep that racket up all night? I wonder you get any sleep.'

'I've slept in worse places.'

They exchanged a look. Then Boulter tipped back the mug, finished, banged it on the table. 'Be seeing you, Jim. And thanks for the coffee. Biscuits next time, OK? Choccy ones for preference.'

'Just close the door after you.'

Boulter left it open and stamped downstairs.

'Shit!' Jim smashed a fist into a palm. 'Of all the . . . *Now*, when I'm ready to . . .'

But he wasn't. Not exactly. He had to wait until his face healed and he was already waiting for the twelfth.

Then he began to see an advantage in it. If Boulter talked to Eric Shaw, then when Jim suddenly left the job it would seem to be connected to that. He sucked at one of the raw patches on the hand he'd crushed between the boats. Yes, Boulter's arrival in his life might prove convenient. Anyway, it had happened. Best to stop worrying over it and let events unfold. He went back to sleep.

In the early evening he listened to the local radio news but there was nothing about Matthew Reynoldes. He was driving the van back to Acton at the time and when the bulletin ended he sought a callbox and rang Penny. Mrs Reynoldes answered, her voice thick. She didn't ask who he was, she asked him to hold.

'Jim?' Penny's voice was tiny, she seemed vulnerable.

'Hi there. How are you?' But he knew already.

'Oh Jim, it's dreadful. My father, he's dead.'

He went into a sequence of mystification, sympathy, shock, regret. She had no chance of knowing it was an act.

'A heart attack,' she explained. 'They found him in his car by the river, but the terrible thing is somebody had been into the car and stolen stuff. Can you believe anything so callous? He was sitting there, dead or dying, and some monster was ransacking the car.'

He heard her sobbing. He found words. Not comfort, that wasn't possible. She sniffed and apologized for breaking down. Only the English, he thought, would consider it a failing.

Penny said: 'I've got to go, that was the doorbell. It's been like this all day, people popping round to see if we're all right or ringing up to say how sorry they are.' She sniffed. 'Perhaps in a day or two, when things have calmed down a bit . . . It would be nice to get out for a while.'

'Sure, I'll call you.' In the background he could hear her doorbell.

He delivered the van, slipped the keys through the letter-box and went to catch a train home. The Matthew Reynoldes

61

poster smiled at him. How long before they replaced it with a different face smiling a different smile of reassurance?

Sunset at Willesden. He dallied on the platform as the train pulled out. Beneath the grey slate and red-tile roofs of Tubbs Road a window pane flared orange. Criss-crossing railway lines shone like polished cutlery, and the red and blue paint of the station's woodwork was as jolly as a child's toy. Jim picked out his own window. He couldn't see a face at it, but he waved anyway.

For two more days he stayed off work. By then the scratches were fading and a pair of sunglasses concealed his damaged eye. Eric Shaw didn't comment on his appearance and neither did he mention the police. Jim was glad to be away from Tubbs Road because Geordie was needling Stefan and Stefan's response was to mope in Jim's room.

Jim went to see Penny. He invented a car crash, to explain his injuries and his arrival on foot. She'd been stuck in the house and was keen to go out, but Jim preferred to stay there and won. Penny poured them drinks on the terrace. Her mother was out but came home after an hour and Penny suggested the three of them had supper in the garden. She went inside to wash salad, leaving Jim and her mother to talk.

Mrs Reynoldes said: 'I'm afraid I was rather muddled when I first met you, mixing you up with a man who was supposed to give an estimate for hanging a balcony outside the bedroom window.' She laughed at her stupidity. 'Actually it wasn't until Penny told me you'd become friends that I realized my mistake. The other man never turned up you see.'

He didn't want to discuss this but there was no ducking the question she raised next. Why had he been there? Jim jiggled the ice in his drink and gave her the answer that had satisfied Penny. 'Your husband was considering having a satellite dish.'

'He was *what*?' She recovered, modified her reaction. 'I'm sorry but I'd say that was the last thing to interest him. Well, at any rate he never mentioned it to me.'

He was about to take them off the topic when she asked: 'Did you know him?'

'I saw him around Richmond.'

And then she told him about Reynoldes's exacting working life, the pressures on his time and the effect on his health, culminating in the premature heart attack his doctor had feared. She said: 'Matthew wouldn't listen, wouldn't go along with the advice about slowing down.'

Most of her conversation was like that, supplying Jim with banal background. Penny was his informant about the fisherman who'd gone along the towpath early in the morning and discovered the body, and about the police being involved because there were unusual factors. He hoped for more but it was the end of the evening before the subject revived and she said that the car's tax disc, in its plastic cover, had been found on the bank a mile from the car.

'It was new,' she said. 'Nearly a full year's tax and yet whoever was ghoulish enough to steal it threw it away. There really are some crazy people out there.'

Then she glanced at her mother, felt the remark was ill judged, and busied herself with the coffee pot. Matthew Reynoldes wasn't mentioned again.

Penny said goodbye to Jim in the courtyard. 'Ring me soon, Jim. Mummy's sister's coming tomorrow to spend a couple of weeks with her so I won't feel so trapped in the house then. I should be able to go out at the weekend.'

But he had other plans.

When he got home a letter was on his table. He ran down to interrupt Stefan's television viewing. Stefan, adjusting with maddening slowness from crime in Miami to reality in Willesden, blinked at the envelope in Jim's hand. Then: 'Oh yes, sorry Jim. I brought it upstairs but I must have put it down in here by mistake and forgotten it.' He swept greasy dark hair out of his eyes and repeated: 'Sorry.'

He was so incompetent it was hard to know what to say. Jim muttered that it wasn't important, it didn't matter, that he'd just wondered what had happened. Alone, upstairs again, he reread the letter. It was dated five weeks ago. The signature was large and swirly although not easy to decipher as characters were glossed over. But Matthew Reynoldes had sent him his apology.

He sat on the edge of the bed, head in his hands, shaking with laughter. *Because of Stefan*, Matthew Reynoldes was dead!

Choosing a time when the customer was outside watering her shrubs, Jim asked to use the telephone. He called a London hotel and booked a suite. The hotel believed he was the personal assistant of an American industrialist and that the suite was for the use of the man's son.

Jim drove to another job. As he carried out the simple routines, he ran through the details he'd learned by rote from the newspaper cuttings. The game was about to begin.

He arrived at the hotel by taxi, wearing his new Italian suit and carrying an expensive suitcase. From the moment he met deference in the eyes of the doorman, he knew with absolute confidence that people were going to play by his rules. When he was shown the suite he grunted, in an educated New York accent, that it was just fine, and he accepted an offer of help with his unpacking. The offer pleased him, confirming that there was no service that would be withheld. He listened to the girl sliding drawers in the bedroom, and then lifted the receiver and made his first call as James B. Orlando, junior.

This was to a man who shared a special interest with the younger Mr Orlando. 'I may possibly have something to interest you, Mr Quincey, sir. Would you care to come by, tomorrow say, around four?'

Whatever Quincey's plans were for Saturday he dropped them and said yes.

Jim asked the hotel reception clerk for a chauffeur-driven limousine to be made available for him from eleven next day. He had them send up an early supper and he went into the jet-lag routine, booking a morning call and asking not to be disturbed before then.

The real James B. Orlando was on his way to Sarawak jungle while Jim was bandying his name in London. He was a reticent young man who'd spent his twenty-eight years dodging photographers and all but essential social contact. When he travelled, as his interests obliged him to do, he protected his privacy by demanding discretion from those around him. There were two supreme pleasures in his life: orchids and alcohol.

Jim poured a drink from the supply in the room, emptied two other miniatures down the washbasin and tossed the bottles into the wastebin. After an hour he asked room service for a bottle of Scotch. When it came, he tipped away around four inches.

This was the dull part, the hours when nothing was to be done. Jim watched a video and a late film on television, but his hand kept straying to what he called his Orlando file, a fine leather Filofax with JBO in gold lettering on the cover. Diary entries, notes and other documents were in an approximation of Orlando's mean neat handwriting. In slots inside the back cover the edges of a row of credit cards were visible.

Eventually he went to bed, the Filofax beside a jumble of dollar bills and small US change on the table where it would be noticed by the man who brought breakfast. Jim was on the telephone when he came, apparently telling a friend in England that he was based in London for a few weeks but would be making a short trip to Paris. He arranged to visit the friend on Wednesday. There was no one on the line.

After breakfast he went out, the doorman ushering him into a waiting taxi that took him to Knightsbridge. During the morning he gathered charge cards from stores and ordered them to send purchases to the hotel. In the afternoon he bought clothes, formal and sportswear, and the limousine met him outside one of the shops and carried him to the hotel in time for his appointment with Quincey. It was all so easy.

Quincey was invited up to his suite. Jim was on the telephone again, to reception with a query. Jim's end of the conversation was oblique, misleading.

'New York,' Jim apologized as he set the receiver down. 'I've asked that we're not interrupted again.'

The cuttings had told him about Quincey too, a brindled sort of man, greyish-brown jacket, greyish-brown hair that appeared to grow vertical from his scalp. He looked like a caricature of a bumbling English eccentric, but he was no fool. Especially not where orchids were concerned.

Quincey chose one of the velvet Edwardian chairs. Jim noted he was leaning forward a fraction, expectant. Good, he thought, he's ready to be hooked.

'I can't tell you,' began Quincey, 'how delighted I was to receive your telephone call, Mr Orlando. Delighted and astonished.'

Jim looked as diffident as the genuine Orlando might have done. 'Well now, Mr Quincey, I hope you're not going to be disappointed.'

'No, no, I'm sure of it.'

'We-ell, I guess you ought to hear exactly what it is I'm offering.'

Offering was the only word Quincey cared to notice. He inclined some more, a tongue licked his underlip.

Jim said: 'I'll come to the point, Mr Quincey. You and I are both collectors, both with a certain standing I might say . . .'

Quincey was nodding, agreement and encouragement.

'. . . and we both know what a tough world it's turned into since we started out. You more than me, of course, as you've been involved longer.'

Quincey was fifty. The nodding became more vigorous and he growled: 'All those cursed restrictions.' He meant efforts at protecting the future of the species through conservation, but neither Quincey nor James B. Orlando, junior, could be expected to see it that way.

Jim agreed. 'And that's why . . .'

There was a tap at the door. Jim had been expecting it. Tea was served. He was in no hurry to resume but the sweat broke on Quincey's forehead. As soon as the waiter withdrew Jim went on: 'I'm offering you a *Paphiopedilum Orlandianum*, Mr Quincey.' He scarcely paused for the man's sharp intake of breath and continued: 'I have three from my last expedition and it would please me to help one other expert extend his collection of slipper orchids as I have completed mine.'

Quincey was overwhelmed. 'An Orlandianum! This is too generous.'

Diffidence again. 'Oh, I don't know about that. It's my view that this is something the collections must have. And if anything were to happen to my own collection, in the future I mean when I might no longer be in control of its destiny . . .' Here a self-mocking laugh. 'I guess it's no secret that the rest of my family fail to share my hobby. In fact, they think it's the craziest thing they ever heard.'

Quincey grasped the hint. 'But surely they'd never destroy the Orlando collection?'

Jim was ready to backtrack. 'No, I don't say they'd do that. But you know the way it goes, we can none of us be certain how our things will be disposed of. Maybe they wouldn't deliberately destroy, but negligence creeps in when people undervalue a thing. Don't you agree?'

Quincey obliged by nodding.

'And you,' said Jim, 'are to leave your collection to the British nation, sir.'

'Indeed, that *is* my intention. Despite all the difficulties that are laid in the way of collectors in these awkward times, this nation remains very happy to accept gifts.' A mite pompously he elaborated on the intended destination of the Quincey collection. Jim already knew but heard him out.

After tea, which led them along the byways of the orchid world, they came to the crux. Money. Quincey was asked to pay a horrifying amount. The nodding came to an end, he receded in the chair. When he said: 'Ah,' it was no longer craving, it was lament.

But Jim knew Quincey could afford it. 'I can give you time,' he said. 'I shall be in London for a few days yet. But I would appreciate an early answer, Mr Quincey, sir.'

'Of course, of course. But that's a lot of money, Mr Orlando, a lot of money.'

'For an Orlandianum?'

'Hmm,' said Quincey, getting to his feet too.

Jim called reception and asked whether there were any messages. Quincey heard the end of the conversation that pretended there were. Jim hung up, read the time.

'I have to drive over to Kensington,' he said. 'May I drop you somewhere?' Quincey's London flat was out that way.

Quincey accepted, anticipating a taxi ride and failing to be unimpressed as the chauffeur opened the door of the limousine. On the journey Jim tossed in an idea about handing over the entire Orlando collection to a fellow collector, rather than risk the disaster of an uncaring family.

Quincey was incredulous. 'Are you saying you might give it away?'

Jim shrugged. 'Oh, I've really no idea. I haven't seriously thought about it at all. And it could be a long way off.'

'Well, yes.' Quincey gave a chuckle that threatened to choke him. 'You're a young man, Mr Orlando. You have years of collecting ahead of you.'

'Not so very many. One or two gaps, you understand, sir. And then? Well, I don't know.'

'I see.'

'Yes, I'm a hunter-gatherer at heart, Mr Quincey. The search is the thing, and when I've found everything I've been searching for then I might want to move on and seek out something quite different.'

Quincey repeated his amazement that a collector could consider passing on his collection to another, and possibly for free.

'That would depend,' said Jim, as though thinking aloud. 'A free gift might be the smartest move if it were to go to a man who'd ensure its safety for posterity.'

Beside him he sensed the nodding starting up once more. After the earlier references to his own collection, Quincey imagined himself the likeliest recipient. But he couldn't help blurting out his other thought: 'If your collection went on the market, Mr Orlando, it would be worth a fortune.'

'I guess I already have one of those,' said Jim. And there was nothing to gainsay him.

Before they reached the flat, Jim returned to another strand of their hotel-room conversation. Quincey's collection had duplicates of a few rare items too. Jim felt, by the time the chauffeur was letting Quincey out on to the pavement, that the seed of a scheme had been planted. In all probability Quincey would call him next day.

The limousine went on a few miles. Jim kept it at the kerbside while he shopped in another expensive store and then the chauffeur loaded his parcels into the car. After that they returned to the hotel.

From the list in the JBO Filofax Jim selected another number. But the man's wife answered and said that he was away that weekend. Jim hung up.

The first setback. Minor, or maybe not. Too early to say. There were other collectors, but they weren't all in London or close to it. Nor were they as rich and as greedy as Quincey, nor as unscrupulous about the origins of their specimens. Jim's real target was Quincey but he wanted another buyer primed if Quincey needed to be pushed.

All right, then. What about Ramshaw? He wasn't ideal but he might be in London and it was possible he'd do instead of the man inconveniently out of town. Jim prowled the suite, calculating. Ramshaw was very old and Jim believed he was lame. Hadn't that been Ramshaw he'd seen on television months ago being helped into St Martin-in-the-Fields for a well-known botanist's memorial service?

Jim drank a small whisky, against his judgement that was arguing his reasoning was sounder without it. He left half of the measure in the glass, anyway, forgetting it because his mind was on James B. Orlando and the degree of the man's eccentricity. Certainly Orlando was odd enough to put to Quincey a proposition that was a mix of extraordinary generosity to a rival and at the same time an attempt to claw in the dollars. The clippings showed that Orlando had on occasion let it be known that he might sell a specimen, and that his price had proved prohibitive.

Such was the talk of the trade. And yet he would never be ignored because trailing up mountains and through jungles reaped plants that few collectors ever saw in the wild. Like a number of people obsessed with the rare, Orlando owned two kinds of specimens: the honestly acquired and the illegal. The very devil of it, from the authorities' point of view, was proving that acquisition had been illegal.

Flipping a coin, Jim gambled on Ramshaw. The next set-back: Ramshaw was too unwell to speak on the telephone. Jim told a female voice that he was James B. Orlando, junior and wished to converse with Mr Ramshaw as a fellow orchid lover. That made the difference. Ramshaw rallied.

As Jim had feared, involving Ramshaw meant taking the game on to the man's home territory. Jim went in the limousine. The woman he'd spoken to was not, as he'd guessed, a nurse but was Ramshaw's niece, a comfortably untidy young woman with long floppy hair. The old man called her Nellie. Details of Ramshaw's ménage were beyond Jim's research, the episode was risky. Nellie stayed in the room during most of the discussion, leaving only when her uncle effectively asked her to because he detected business that wouldn't surface in her presence.

Afterwards, Ramshaw leaned back on his pillows and shut his eyes for a long time. At first Jim thought he was contemplating, and maybe it began that way. But eventually Jim crept out of the room. Nellie was coming upstairs.

Jim said: 'I believe he's asleep, Miss Ramshaw.'

She had one of those smiles that make guests linger. Jim lingered, over a drink in a rumpled sitting room, and then she excused herself for a few minutes to return, excited, saying her uncle had explained about the offer. 'We're rather flattered, you know, that you should think of us.'

We? Nellie Ramshaw's subsequent remarks underlined that impression: she shared her uncle's passion and worked with him on the collection now that he was failing. Jim hadn't bargained for this. An ailing old man like Ramshaw or an avaricious one like Quincey suited his purpose better than a keen-witted woman in her thirties.

As he drove back across London he wrote her name in Orlando's prissy handwriting in the Filofax. Nellie Ramshaw knew where he was staying. Unfortunate, but he'd had to offer her scraps of information over the whisky and he wasn't up to a detailed chat about orchids, not with a young woman unclouded by covetousness. Rather than make a slip, he'd played the American tourist impressed with the shops and asking after the best restaurants.

He'd offered the identical plant to Quincey and Ramshaw, because that kept it simple. It was a specimen Orlando had discovered and named after himself. Not until Jim's visit to Quincey had anyone ever heard of Orlando owning more than one of them.

Quincey rang in the morning, early, then hummed and hawed before getting to a tentative proposition: how would it be if he were to meet part of the cash price and provide a plant of his own as the balance? He mentioned another highly sought-after orchid.

Jim displayed reluctance. They juggled the figures somewhat, to Jim's advantage. And then Jim asked to be allowed a while to think it over. Ringing off, he pictured Quincey frantic, afraid of rejection, scared that if he didn't reach a deal he'd jeopardize that other splendid prospect, possession of the entire Orlando collection.

An hour later Jim called him back. 'OK,' he said, with the faintest sigh to emphasize that he knew he was being too altruistic. 'We have a deal.'

Quincey's joy came in a rush of words, about the mechanics of getting the money into Jim's hand and about the quality of the plant he was to provide. He was gabbling, his voice high and his excitement spiralling.

Jim said: 'We have to be a little careful here.' Obliquely he was conceding that Orlandianums were stolen and smuggled plants.

'Ah, indeed.' The illegality sufficed to hold the spiral steady.

Jim said: 'It would be safest for us to avoid meeting again.'

'Then how?'

'And I would suggest, if I may, that a cheque from you to me might arouse suspicions where we would both prefer none were stirred.'

Quincey had control at last. 'Quite. Cash then? Of course, it'll take a day or two.'

'Call me when you have it, Mr Quincey. We'll go right on from there.'

And then he danced about the room and punched the air.

Gleeful laughter erupted. God, the effort of playing quiet, shy James B. Orlando was stifling!

Jim whipped open the wardrobe door. In the bottom he'd piled the packages bought on his spree. He tore off wrappers, hung up clothes. The precious things – jewellery, watches, cigarette lighters and pens – he left in presentation boxes, except for a handful which he removed with care so that their empty boxes could be rewrapped. These empty ones he entrusted to the hotel safe.

Sunday was a bad day for most kinds of business but his next step wasn't hindered. He crammed the goods in a briefcase, left by a side door and hailed a taxi. A rabbinical-looking gentleman in a green-tiled house in Hampstead Garden Suburb gave him a fair price for the stuff. Nothing near the shop price but something to celebrate all the same. Caged in the hotel once more, Jim ordered champagne.

There was a fleeting moment of despair after the waiter withdrew leaving him with his bottle and solitary glass. Jim didn't especially enjoy champagne and recognized the pathos of drinking it alone. But it was open, he must taste it even if the rest was destined for the washbasin. As he tilted the bottle over the glass, the telephone rang.

'This is reception, Mr Orlando. We have a Miss Ramshaw here for you.'

He had half a second to decide what the hell to do with Nellie Ramshaw. 'Thank you. Please ask her if she'd care to come up.'

He was dismayed. She'd want to inspect a plant he didn't have, she could trap him if she were suspicious and she could let him blunder into revealing his ignorance if she were not. More, she was a woman who believed she'd encountered a millionaire who shared her obsession and was, unlike the majority of millionaires, young and personable. Oh yes, Jim feared Nellie Ramshaw and his fear grew with every step she took on her way to his suite.

She had spruced herself up. His worries deepened. Yesterday she'd been at home and dressed for that. Today she'd taken some trouble and presumably on his account. There was an upswept hairstyle, a silk dress, a few gold chains twisted around her throat. Maybe the dress could have been buttoned two or three inches higher, maybe the belt needn't have been cinched so tight. The effect wasn't tarty, it was the contrast with the jeans and T-shirt of the previous day that jangled his nerves.

He was welcoming, ordered another glass, watched her arrange herself in the same velvet chair where Quincey had sat. She had good legs, not long but neat. He waited for the rest of her message.

She set her glass on the ornate table beside her and rested her hands in her lap. 'We're thinking very seriously about your offer, Mr Orlando. But we'd like further information.'

'You'd like to see the plant. Of course you would. Perhaps I ought to have mentioned yesterday that I don't have it at the hotel. It's in the care of a friend near Oxford. Safer, you see. But go right ahead, ask anything else you need to know.'

Her face fell at the news that the plant wasn't to hand, but the danger of keeping a valuable specimen in a hotel room didn't need amplification. She said: 'I told you my uncle and I are flattered that you thought of coming to us, but the truth is we're also puzzled. There are other collectors who could more readily meet your price, people such as Quincey or . . .'

'Quincey.' He spoke the name with a dismissive curl of the lip.

'I see.'

'Sure I know about Quincey. The man has a fine collection but why would I wish to assist Quincey?'

Nellie Ramshaw tipped her head in agreement. 'My uncle has always said Quincey could bring the entire game into disrepute. Quincey has raised eyebrows at Kew, you know. For my uncle, you see, regulations are there to be obeyed. He comes from that sort of background – army, civil service.'

'Rule makers, not rule breakers?'

She smiled. 'Precisely.'

He topped up her glass. Close, he breathed her summery perfume. He said: 'Have I answered your question?'

'About Quincey, yes. But that's just part of it. We're also curious to know whether you've made other approaches.'

He drank, watching her over the rim of his glass, a gleam

73

of amusement in his eyes as he kept her dangling until her temerity embarrassed her. Then he said: 'I guess I'm not actually conducting an auction. I've discussed this with only two people.'

Her hope died. She bit a lip, then forced a rueful smile. All along it had been too much to imagine that the Ramshaw collection would enjoy the beneficence of Orlando. And yet hope is inevitably spent on improbabilities.

Jim told her. 'I've spoken to Mr Ramshaw and to his niece.'

She burst out laughing, delighted. But when she spoke she was cautious. 'It's a lot of money. To us, I mean. Oh don't think I'm pleading poverty, but you've seen my uncle's state of health. There are medical bills, nurses, all kinds of demands on what he has.'

So, she was opening negotiations. Jim expected to clinch a deal with her within half an hour and to be asked to await confirmation from her uncle. She adhered to the course he predicted.

The Ramshaws were asked a considerably lower fee than the one he had exacted from Quincey, and Jim allowed Nellie Ramshaw the satisfaction of beating him down a respectable amount. Like Quincey, she offered an orchid in part-payment. As the Ramshaw collection contained nothing worth adding to Orlando's their orchid was to be sold on. Nellie gave Jim the choice of waiting for her to sell it or else taking the plant himself. He chose to take it from her.

When she had gone he was disquieted to see that the champagne bottle was two-thirds empty, and anxious that alcohol had made him careless. But picking over the general chatter and the transaction he couldn't see a flaw. And that pin-pointed the problem. His knowledge of orchid collecting was scant, if he made a gaffe he'd never know it.

He ordered coffee, to clear his mind. She was meant to telephone that evening with, they both hoped, her uncle's approval.

The call didn't come. Jim fidgeted, watched television, fretted. He told himself to forget it, that it didn't matter, that the real prey was Quincey and that Quincey had been snared. Yet his qualms about Ramshaw's niece persisted: her silence could mean anything *except* that her uncle had rubber-stamped the terms Jim had agreed with her. He pictured the worst, that she was suspicious and checking with Quincey and other collectors whether they'd been approached by a man claiming to be James B. Orlando.

Early next day, Monday, he left the hotel carrying a small case that contained some of his older clothes. He changed into them at Paddington then travelled to Acton and worked all day for J. and J. Electrical. In the evening he went to Tubbs Road, contrived to say a word or two to Geordie and had a short chat with Stefan before pleading a headache and saying he was going to take painkillers and lie down. Once Stefan was downstairs, and the television had established that he was watching a soap opera, Jim slipped out of the house and returned to the hotel. There were several messages for Orlando, one from Quincey and the rest from Nellie Ramshaw.

Jim spoke first to Quincey. The man was warning of a delay in raising the full amount of cash. Wary, Jim decided against revising their plan. In truth he was annoyed that Quincey seemed to think he was foolish enough to hand over an Orlandianum on receipt of Quincey's inferior orchid plus only part of the money. He told Quincey he was flying to Paris at the weekend and urged him to settle the matter by then. There was a strong hint that if Quincey missed the deadline, the deal was off.

Next the Ramshaws. Jim's hand shook as he dialled the number. Nellie's tone of voice allayed fear. 'Oh thank you *so* much for calling back. I was getting desperate when I couldn't reach you today.'

He pointed out: 'I have a heavy schedule, Miss Ramshaw. Our arrangement was for you to call yesterday evening, if you remember.'

'Yes, I know. And I'm very sorry I didn't, but when I came home I discovered my uncle was worse and I had to . . .'

He lost interest in the minutiae of it, the point was that Ramshaw had now recovered sufficiently to say yes. Quincey and Ramshaw, he'd won all round. They'd bought it, and all he wanted now was the money.

A couple of evenings later Nellie Ramshaw sat in the red velvet chair and held out to him the package from her handbag. He gestured to her to unwrap it. The paper fell back, revealing the dull leaves and straggly roots of what, under the right conditions, would become a spectacular slipper orchid with petals resembling pink and mauve ribbons. She raised her eyes to his, keen to see his reaction. He adopted the doting look of the devotee.

Yet there was a chance that she had doubts about him. Cunningly, Jim didn't speak, neither to praise the plant (which for all he knew might be worthless, a trick to test him) nor to criticize it. He reached towards her and she handed the package. Jim peered at it and lay it on the table.

'Mine's still in Oxford,' he confessed. And as an oh of disappointment broke from her he hurried on. 'At least, my friend is on his way to deliver it. I'd say it should be here any time.'

He suggested a drink while they waited. Then he pretended to try the friend's Oxford telephone number and reported that he couldn't get through. As time drew on, he offered her supper.

They ate in the hotel restaurant, ostensibly because the Oxford friend would be able to find them there. But before their coffee was served, Jim left the restaurant and returned angry and apologetic with the news that the hotel staff had failed to pass on a message saying that his friend's car had been in an accident and the man couldn't come to London that evening after all.

Nellie Ramshaw helped by switching her disappointment into concern for the possibly injured friend and offering assurances that the delay didn't matter. He promised to send his driver to her uncle's house with the cutting without fail next day. Jim knew enough about her life to be certain she'd be busy then and unable to chase round to the hotel. Seeing his distress and embarrassment, she brushed aside his apparent insistence that she take her own plant home with her.

His crowded diary illustrated how difficult it was going to be for them to meet again that week, but the thing most in his favour was that old Ramshaw had set his heart on the

Orlandianum and Nellie had set her heart on getting it for her uncle as soon as possible. She took a taxi home, confident that James B. Orlando's chauffeur would be on her doorstep next day and that it was perfectly reasonable to leave the Ramshaw plant and the Ramshaw cheque, made out to cash 'for tax reasons', with the handsome young American millionaire.

He was one of the most interesting men she'd met in years and she'd enjoyed her evening although she'd drunk more than usual, mainly because of the time wasted waiting for the unfortunate friend from Oxford. They had a tentative arrangement to have dinner together in a week's time. He'd said he'd call her about that. Nellie Ramshaw fully expected that was true too.

Four

Jim's Aunt Maria, the one who wore corsets and played the organ in the white-painted church, was proud that the family came of English stock. Pride was her special sin. She was proud of her fine upright appearance, proud of her dominant role in family life, proud to be getting more off her acres than her neighbours managed.

Her brother grouched. 'Didn't nobody ever tell Maria that pride is a deadly sin?'

No one answered him. He said: 'Maria is a darned proud woman.' And he shook his head, took up his knife and made another score down a length of heavy dark hide. Some men took to drink and some men took to religion but he'd taken to making leather belts.

Maria said to Jim: 'When you're grown, boy, you want to be sure to marry into good English stock.'

Jim was standing beside her as she sat. He was scuffing the toe of his left shoe against his right calf where there was an itch he couldn't trouble to bend down for. He screwed up his face. 'Why?'

'Because that's the quality, Jim. That's why.'

He didn't understand. He tried to shape a question. But she said: 'I'm ready. Are you following this time?'

Jim stood to attention and took a breath. Maria raised her arms from her lap, clawed her hands and leaned forward from the waist. She was a predator going for the kill. Her hands swooped. A chord rang out. Another. One more. Then she brought in the melody.

Beside her, Jim pumped the organ. He'd be glad when the

electric organ was fixed and this relic could once more be regarded as antique ornament.

He pumped and he pondered. Good English stock? He was a farm boy, he knew stock was animals, cows mainly. He pumped and he planned to beg his father to let him go to market so he could check up on what English stock was exactly. And if he was to choose a wife from a family that farmed these cattle, then he wanted a good look at the girls too. But how likely was it that they'd be at the market?

Maria swung her head from the page of music and fixed her eyes on Jim, urging him on. She sang at him:

> Are you Shining for Jesus, my brother,
> Shining for truth and for right . . .

So close, her age-mottled face scared him pleasantly. Her head was bobbing and her whole body rocking to the tumpty-tumpty-tum of the hymn.

> Where bold unbelief and its minions
> Are posing as angels of light?

The organ wheezed on the final verse, as his arms were aching. Maria turned to another page and ran a finger down the lines of black squiggles in which the tunes were disguised. Then she registered the plaintive appeal on his face. She flipped the hymn book shut.

'You're too weak to be Joe's boy. I don't know where Ellen got you.'

She picked up her handbag, stood, shook out her long skirts. 'When Joe was a boy he could carry a bale of hay and never notice it.'

'Did he pump the organ for you too?'

She pursed her lips. 'No, I can't say he ever did that.'

They went out of the church. People going by in a van waved at them but Jim knew they were laughing too. Maria was much older than his father, her clothes were old-fashioned and so were her ways. People called her quaint.

Back at her place she showed him a book. 'I can't get Joe interested in this but it's my duty to see that you know about it. So you listen, Jim.'

He wriggled closer on his chair to prove attention. Maria opened the book on the pine table where they could both see it. His reading was shaky, he relied on her.

The book was an odd one, a guide book although he didn't know that. She said her mother had shown it to her when she was a girl. 'You see this?'

He made out 'Rushwood, Norfolk'.

Maria said: 'This is about a manor – that means a real good place: smart house, a fine parcel of land – in England. The folks that live there are also called Rushwood. Maybe the manor was named after them, maybe t'other way round. It don't say.' She peered at the page. 'They're connected, Jim.'

She spun the book out of his reach and re-opened it at the back. A spare page had been filled with handwritten names linked to each other with short straight lines.

Maria jabbed a finger at the top of the page. 'Starts right here with somebody name of Wilfred Rushwolde on that land before ever they wrote up the Domesday Book.'

She pronounced it 'dome' instead of 'doom'. Jim had never heard of it either way. She said: 'The family has been around that manor ever since.'

'Is that good?'

'That's good for sure, boy. And look at this . . .' She was smoothing her finger along the lines in search of something special.

Jim asked: 'What about before Wilfred?'

'Eh?'

'Where did Wilfred's ma and pa live?'

'I guess nobody thought to ask that. Now, see this name? This is a very famous name. Walter Rushwynde. Jim, that was a man who wrote poetry to a queen. Think of that, Jim.'

Jim thought. He didn't think it so very impressive. 'Was he famous for that?'

'More because she cut his head off!' A harsh laugh. Her finger poked at another name. 'Now, this one. He was an admiral.'

Admirals didn't figure much in Iowa. Jim could see snags. 'Who looked after the manor while he was being an admiral?'

'Save us, the questions you ask! Servants, that's who.'

Jim had been picturing a smart house to be one that was given an annual lick of paint and had a purpose-built garage instead of a barn to make do. He thought a fine parcel of land would be around what you'd have if you lumped together his father's holding and Aunt Maria's, except that you couldn't do that because of old man Weedon's farm in between. No way had he thought of servants. Rushwood expanded in his imagination. Perhaps if you included the Weedon place too?

Maria was tiring of his stupidity, or maybe her information was skimpy. She hopped to a woman who'd married a royal prince. Then she closed the book, a peculiar state of satisfaction and pride settling on her. 'We're from good English stock, Jim. Right back to Wilfred Rushwolde, that's how far we go.'

At first the concept eluded him. Then he mustered a reply. 'You mean all those people were our family, in history?'

'Sure, that's the way it was.' Maria folded her hands on the cover of the book, exactly as she rested her hands on the Bible in church.

Jim flashed back: 'But why are the names different?'

She was ready for that one. 'They weren't spellers, Jim. People put their names any whichway. Rushwolde. Rushwynde. Rushwood. What did it matter, they knew who was who? Made it their business. They have books in England where you can read up on names.'

'But we're only Rush.'

'I guess the rest of it got in the way. When our ancestors came over here they were too busy to go fussing after extra syllables. Neat and short, that's what they liked.'

She rose, held the book to her black-buttoned bosom. He was finding some other footling objection but she brought the subject to an end with a line spoken like a proverb. 'Go for the big ideas, Jim, and the details will take care of themselves.'

After that there was nothing worth saying.

Matthew Reynoldes's widow was agitated. She stirred her coffee a second time, having forgotten the first. Although she was making an effort to be hospitable, her mind was elsewhere. Her watch slid an inch down her freckled wrist and she pushed it back. There were fine lines, new ones, around her mouth. She'd lost weight since her husband died.

'I can't think where she's got to,' she repeated.

Jim relaxed in the armchair opposite her, brushed a hair from the sleeve of his jacket. 'I guess she'll be along just as soon as she can make it.'

But he was put out. Penny had been keen for him to come over and now she was keeping him waiting. He liked Mrs Reynoldes yet conversation was difficult when she was pre-occupied. Besides, it was Penny who could be relied on to tell him what he needed to know, not her mother. The inquest on Matthew Reynoldes had been opened and adjourned *sine die*, and the local newspaper stated that the police were invest-igating the case as a suspicious death. Jim took that to mean murder. He shivered.

Mrs Reynoldes was quick with an apology. 'Yes, I'm afraid it's growing chilly in here. I think perhaps I'll switch on the . . .' She was rising from her chair.

'No, no, I'm fine. Truly.'

She moved to the window, a fretwork of rain on the glass. 'It's the contrast. Such a wonderful summer, and suddenly . . .' There was a catch in her voice. Such a wonder-ful life, and suddenly she was alone.

Penny came then, ringing the doorbell because she'd mis-laid her key. Jim overheard Mrs Reynoldes's whispered annoyance and Penny's petulant retort before Penny was in the room with him, her colour high and her blonde hair rain-darkened.

'Jim, I'm sorry.' She kissed him, confident of forgiveness.

He fancied she didn't want to explain, that she'd long ago discovered that a smile and a quick peck from a pretty girl managed all things. He asked: 'What happened?'

'Oh, you know. I got held up.' She accompanied this with a flutter of the hand to indicate it was too tedious to go into.

He let her get away with it. 'How about we go down the hill for a drink, get something to eat?'

She was eager, said she'd change her damp clothes and be ready in no time. No time turned out to be ten minutes.

It would have been less if Mrs Reynoldes hadn't pursued her upstairs for more of the subdued argument.

'Phew!' said Penny, immediately she and Jim closed the front door behind them. She pretended to collapse with exhaustion against one of the pillars of the portico.

He laughed. 'Having a bad time?'

She took car keys from her pocket and dangled them in front of him. 'Oh perhaps it's not so very bad.'

She drove them downhill, in what had been her mother's car until her father's death. 'There was going to be a decent car if I passed my exams, but this will have to do by the look of it.' By decent she meant racier. The hand-me-down car was one year old, middle of the market, top of the range.

'You drive well.'

She pretended arrogance. 'Naturally. I do everything well. Pass exams, sing, paint, play sports . . .'

'Hey, your tennis isn't that great. I've seen you in action, and I have to tell you, Penny, your action leaves something to be desired.'

The car slid into a parking space outside a restaurant they'd used before. 'This OK?'

He said yes, to the restaurant and to the skilful parking. Over the first drink he asked her: 'Tell me about the bad time.'

She wrinkled her nose. 'It's just families, Jim. You know how they are. Mummy's getting heaps of conflicting advice – sell the house, keep the house, do this, do that.'

'And what do you think?'

'I say she could keep the Queens Road house, sell the boat-house in Scotland because she won't be able to cope with both as well as her interior design business, and . . .' A sigh. Her sentence fizzled away.

'And?'

'And I should get my share of the boat-house money, go to a crammer in Kensington to get qualifications fast, and get on with my life.'

'Hmm. I bet that's drummed up conflicting advice from the family too.'

'From Mummy mostly. I can see she wants me around,

that it's all coming at the wrong time. But I have to get away before long and the way things have worked out, this is my best chance.'

Jim put his money on Penny. She'd always struck him as a girl who knew how to get what she wanted. If she said it was time to cut loose, then so it was. Provided she got the money. He wondered how much it was.

Penny said: 'Actually, Jim, it's because of all this that I was late. I'm not the only one in the family who wants to get hot little hands on Daddy's money. If Mummy's being obstructive it's because she's blocking someone else. I've been negotiating this evening – pretty delicately, I might say – to see how we can launch a combined attack on Mummy. Nicely, of course. Mummy's very upset.'

Because the food arrived they lost the thread and it was a while later that Jim manoeuvred them to the police inquiry. Penny was matter-of-fact. 'There was bruising, indications that he'd been injured and might have been put into the driving seat after he was dead.'

'What indications?' He was trying to judge a normal degree of interest. He raised his wine glass and drank. Out of sight, his other hand clenched.

Penny said: 'Technical stuff. Oh, you know the way policemen speak, more to confuse than elucidate. But there were head injuries, bruises to his arms, his legs and chest. And they are interested in the mud and grass on his shoes and in the rear passenger footwell. There's an idea it mightn't have come from the riverbank. They are going to run tests to check that.'

Jim frowned, genuinely puzzled. 'Why should they be looking for riverbank mud? Did someone see him walking around there?'

He bridled when her expression showed she thought he was being thick. She said: 'Jim, Daddy's things disappeared from the car and his driving licence floated ashore downriver. Remember? Now, if he'd junked the stuff himself he'd have had to get out of the car to do it. Also they are trying to discover whether he was attacked elsewhere and the car dumped by the river with his body in it after he was dead.'

He was horrified. 'Do they really think that's what happened?'

'The inspector told me it's a possibility, one they have to explore. You must admit it's pretty strange when you add all the peculiarities together.' She checked off points on her fingers. 'The car tax, the most valuable thing, is thrown away; the injuries happened shortly before death; and, oh yes, I forgot to say this but the car was wiped clean. None of Daddy's fingerprints and none of anybody else's.'

The last point excited her so that her voice rose enough to swivel heads at another table. Penny flushed and leaned forward, adding in a lower voice: 'We've been asked whether he had any enemies.'

Jim nearly laughed. *Enemies?* Who did they think Matthew Reynoldes had been? The man worked for British Rail, he had dissatisfied customers, that was all. He struggled with his face.

Penny's gave way to a mischievous smile. 'Isn't it absurd? Makes him sound like a man with a double life. Underworld. Or secret service.'

Jim blessed her for allowing him to smile. A complicated smile that arose partly from the notion of Reynoldes's enemies but also from his own knowledge of the young mistress, Jennifer Blake, in her Twickenham cottage. How would Penny's attitude to her father swing if he let out what he knew? How would Mrs Reynoldes react to it?

Penny continued to be analytical, coping by latching on to the practical progression rather than letting emotion swamp her. She was fascinated by the world of police work that the inquiry was opening up to her.

'There's such a thing,' she said, 'as the Locard principle.'

Jim posed like an attentive student, as he always did when Penny became didactic, determined to share new-found knowledge. 'Locket?'

'*Locard*. He was a French criminologist who established the principle that every contact leaves a trace. Whoever visits the scene of a crime leaves something there and also takes something away.'

Of course he knew the theory, although not the name Locard. He let her go on.

She said: 'Say Daddy was attacked in another place, the park for instance, then the mud and grass on his shoes would come from there. And he could have left fibres from his clothes, possibly a big item like a torn-off button, at the site.'

Mention of a torn-off button sent a thrill of apprehension down his spine. Had a button been ripped off Reynoldes's clothes in the struggle in the park? Jim controlled his voice and asked while refilling Penny's mineral water glass.

'No,' she said, 'that was an example. I didn't mean it literally. But the Locard principle means that there'd be something, however tiny.'

'Well, if you want to know what I think, my guess is that your father had a fall, died in his car afterwards of a heart attack and some callous bastard stole the trivia he kept in there.'

Penny was impatient with that. 'It won't do. The inspector told me they suspect the things were removed to make it *appear* as though that's what happened. He doesn't believe in the theft, you see. Can't remember when a thief rifling a car troubled to wipe over every surface. He says it doesn't ring true.'

Caution stopped Jim pushing her further. It was unfortunate that the police hadn't fallen for the 'evidence' of the car theft, but he was certain it didn't matter. They could scour Richmond Park for months before they hit on the exact spot where the fight took place, and any fibres from Reynoldes's clothes would have long been washed away by the rain or dispersed by the wind. For all Penny's enthusiasm for police methods, Jim expected the inquiry to peter out, a suspicious death remaining suspicious, nothing more conclusive.

She bubbled on, about things that weren't of much interest to him. Guarded about appearing to pry into the Reynoldes family affairs, he sat through a résumé of her ambitions for the future and her boredom with school. He realized there was another factor, that her chatter was blotting out the thing that was really on her mind. If she hadn't drunk so very little, swilling her wine down with water, he'd have said she was slightly drunk.

When they left, the rain was heavy. Penny leaped into the driving seat and fiddled with the heater controls to demist the windscreen. 'You left your car near the house, right?'

He'd bought a secondhand Ford, in his own name, using what he thought of as his Orlando cash. It was under the trees down Queens Road. She started up the hill but as they neared the roundabout she said: 'Jim, if you're not in a hurry there's somewhere I want to go.'

'Sure.' But his misgivings grew as she left Queens Road on her left and ran down Star and Garter Hill. Well before she joined Petersham Road he was screaming inside his head for her to stop, to turn back. And once she'd joined the road he was desperate for her to pass the entrance to River Place, to be going anywhere but the place he knew must be their destination.

Penny Reynoldes pulled on the handbrake and cut the engine exactly where he'd parked her father's car with the man lying dead on the back seat. She sighed, not the world-weary kind of sigh she'd used to comment on the tiresomeness of life at home, but a forlorn sigh.

He asked: 'This was the place?' The screaming inside had ended, there was fearful emptiness. He knew Penny, he understood her, flattered himself it was so. And yet this had taken him by storm. She'd brought him to the spot he'd chosen for the cover-up – the *failed* cover-up.

'Yes. This is it.' Her voice was small. 'I feel . . .' She didn't know how to go on.

He swallowed, grabbed control of the situation now that she'd lost it. 'Tell me, Penny. *What* do you feel?'

She answered obliquely. 'When something important has happened in a place – something terrible or something wonderful – shouldn't it leave a kind of imprint? I mean, how can intense emotion be expended without leaving any trace? It doesn't. And human beings are diminished by that.'

He swept a hand over condensation on the sidescreen. 'How many times have you come down here?'

He waited until, barely audible, she said: 'About six.'

'Well, I guess if you don't have any playback yet you're not going to get any.' He cursed the rain, wished they could get out and walk a while beside the river.

'It's become my way of mourning. I have to be strong at home because of Mummy, she's broken up. So I come down here. My ritual.'

'You come alone?' The image of her at the riverside seeking a sign disturbed him.

'Until this time. At first I asked Mummy but she couldn't face it. *I* couldn't avoid it. I had to see, to feel whatever there was to feel.' The blonde hair trembled, the slightest shake, before she whispered: 'But I feel nothing.'

The breath-misted windscreen obscured the surge of the river ahead but in their quietness he could hear it. His arm was resting along the back of her seat, he stroked her hair as one might comfort a hurt child. Penny moved towards him, urgently, her mouth intent on his, her tongue entering.

Her mood, her hunger, astonished him. He resisted her, refusing to obey the come-on signals that invited him as far as a man might go.

It would have been easy to have given in to physical demands, his and hers, even the limited space of the car didn't rule it out. But he playfully rejected her, turned down her murmured hint that they get into the back of the car.

When she drew away there was a sulky silence. He did up a button. 'Look, Penny . . .' Something needed to be said, he hadn't a clue what.

'No. I'm sorry.'

But she sounded angry. A rejection was a rejection, however gentle. She opened the car door and stepped out into the rain. Jim couldn't see where she'd got to, he was afraid of her blundering into the river, heightened emotion making her reckless. He went after her.

Penny was on the path, a few yards to the right and watching the water. He ran to her. She shook his hand from her arm. 'Leave me alone. I want to be on my own, can't you understand that?'

'Nobody wants to be on their own in this.' The rain was slashing across the river at them. He spun her round, trapping her protesting arms inside him. 'This is crazy. Get in the car.'

'No. No, I mean it. I want to be by myself.'

But she let him lead her. He pushed her into the passenger seat. Her key was in the ignition and he reversed until it was safe to turn and drive the rest of River Lane. Penny said nothing. The silence now was less sulky than embarrassed. That's what he believed, but she'd been so startling that he was uncertain.

Ostensibly checking traffic before pulling into Petersham Road, he studied her. Rainwater was trickling unchecked through her hair, her dress stuck to her skin and her nipples were shadows beneath cotton. He ignored desire, selected second gear and moved off again. He needed Penny because she was his surest way of finding out about the inquiry into her father's death. If he disappeared from her life, it might be seen as a peculiar thing to be added to all the other peculiarities, especially now that he'd made her quote the detective inspector in detail.

Equally, he was nervous of continuing with her. She was an unwelcome complication while he was deep in the Orlando scam. Enough to juggle life in the West End with work for J. and J. Electrical in Acton without having to fit in a schoolgirl in Richmond too.

Jim balanced the advantages of ditching Penny or keeping up the relationship until the Reynoldes inquiry ran into the sand. He delayed decision. She interrupted his thoughts: 'Don't stop at the house, go down to your car.'

Penny accepted the Ford as a stopgap until repairs were completed on the flashy thing he claimed he'd crashed. But neither of them were interested in this talk about cars.

When he'd parked, swinging her car round to leave her a straight run home, she said: 'Jim, I'm going to tell you something and, well, it's awkward. I don't know whether you'll understand but I have to say it anyway.'

He raised an ironical eyebrow. She'd kept him on the hop all evening, he didn't see how anything she said now could surprise. 'Go right ahead.'

'Well, the thing is . . .' She wasn't looking at him, she was twiddling the tie of her belt.

'Penny?' he obliged her to notice him.

She took a deep breath. 'Right. The thing is, I don't want you to come to the house any more.'

'You're saying you don't want to see me any more?' He found it incredible.

'No, I'm not saying that. I mean, not exactly. Oh dear, I said this was difficult.'

'I'd say you were making yourself clear.' He hadn't meant to be clipped.

She flung the belt down in her lap. 'Listen, please. Mummy's making a big thing about it. You probably heard her going on at me earlier.'

'Now you're saying *she* doesn't want you to see me any more.'

'She doesn't.'

'Oh well, that's fine. You always do what she wants, is that what I'm supposed to believe?'

Penny opened her mouth to speak, lost the words. Then: 'Could I just get to the end of this before you yell at me?'

He got a grip on his feelings, stopped fighting the corner for injured pride and let the rest of the sarcasms go unsaid. 'Sure. I'm listening.'

'Well, she's never been happy about us, partly because she's fond of Clive. Clive's . . .'

'The guy you play tennis with.'

She read more into that remark. 'Yes, OK, tennis and other things besides. Anyway she's happier when I'm going around with Clive, his parents are old friends of hers. And she feels we don't know enough about you. She quizzes me, Jim, and I don't have answers for her. You know what parents are like, they expect their daughters' friends to provide a detailed cv before they go as far as the corner pub for a drink.'

She'd hazarded a joke and he approved it with a weak smile. Penny said: 'It's up to you how much you tell me about yourself, I'm just explaining that it's nothing like enough to satisfy my mother. She thinks it's odd that I never go to your home, that I don't have a phone number for you, that we haven't run across anyone in town who knows you.'

He caught her eye with a wicked smile and drawled Southern-style. 'My, whatever gumshoe she hired did one hell of a bad job on this one.'

Penny squirmed, as he'd intended. 'Sorry, I didn't intend it to sound like that. Spying.'

'I'll bet she even warned you that you could be running around with a married man.'

'You're not, are you?'

'No. Definitely not.'

Penny said: 'And . . .'

'You mean there's more?' It seemed best to be teasing her rather than falling out with her. Whatever happened this evening, there were other days coming when he might need her.

She said: 'Jim, I want to be honest about this. I could have made up an excuse but I prefer the truth. I've told you the background, the rest is that I'm not prepared to let this develop into a big issue at home. The serious thing for me right now is to get my share of the money Daddy left me, go to the crammer and plan for my future.'

Eventually he said: 'All that affection on the riverside just now, I take it that was your way of saying goodbye?' He was laughing at her, wounding. He got out of the car before she found a reply. Then she was out too and calling to him across the roof of the car, just his name.

He saw her face, rain-streaked, distressed, and he continued to laugh. 'Next time you decide to ditch some guy, don't bother with the truth, Penny. Just pretend you're out when he rings. It'll save a whole heap of bother.'

Then he was in the Ford, driving past her and away to the roundabout, then down Richmond Hill and out of town. When his exasperation had settled down to amusement, an intriguing thought came to him. How like Matthew Reynoldes she'd been, how self-centred in pursuit of her own interests.

And then another arresting thought. Penny Reynoldes had endured an unpleasant scene because she trusted in the ultimate decency of telling the truth. She was dropping him but emphasizing that she felt too much for him to tell him a lie. Whereas he'd never treated her to anything but deception.

He accepted she was right to be hard-headed about planning her future, not to let transient boy-girl relationships stand in the way. But he believed she'd go further, that all her life there'd be a goal for which she'd sweep aside other considerations. There'd always been that aspect of Penny, a stain of determination in her character. He had no doubt she'd get where she wanted to go, straight as a dart aimed at a bull's-eye.

Had he liked her? Yes, although she dropped naturally into the past tense as the streets grew humbler and the distance to Willesden shortened. Would he miss her? Yes, but because he'd lost his best means of knowing what the Richmond police were up to.

Never seeing Mrs Reynoldes again troubled him more. She'd impressed him with her mature attractiveness and kind nature. It hurt to learn she didn't like him, didn't trust him. But he had more pressing things on his mind: Nellie Ramshaw, Quincey. His future hinged on the outcome of the Orlando hoax, but he wasn't nervous. He pitied people who couldn't scheme and devise, who were forever at the whim of others or who failed to realize that there were choices to be made.

Jim parked the car a couple of streets from Tubbs Road. He didn't want Geordie or Stefan, or any other neighbours, to know it existed. Stefan came out of his room as Jim went upstairs having picked up mail from the shelf in the passage.

'Hi,' said Jim absently, examining an envelope.

Stefan waited until he drew level, then whispered: 'That man came round again.'

Jim continued the steady movement of sliding his finger beneath the flap. 'Oh, yes? What did he want?'

Stefan gathered a fistful of loose shirt and forced it into his waistband. 'He asked for you. Geordie saw him. I heard them going upstairs.'

Anxiety was admitted by a sharp look. 'Geordie let him into my room?'

'He has keys, for emergencies.'

'Yes, I know all that but . . . Did anything else happen?'

'They were walking around in there.'

Jim thanked Stefan with a pat on the shoulder and ran up to the attic. He hung his jacket in the wardrobe, spacing the hangers, his actions automatic while his mind was on Geordie and what to say to him.

The room was hot. He flung up the sash. A silvery Underground train was slithering out of the station. Lighted carriages hung high in the air on the North London line. A Pullman came wailing from the south. Rain had died, leaving a clean breeze.

Jim shut his eyes, relished coolness on his flesh. He made up his mind to dump the file of newspaper cuttings. The room held no other clues to his secrets. He'd always been clever that way. He left the window open and went downstairs.

Geordie had a can of lager in one hand. It wasn't his first of the evening. His cardigan was corrugated up his back proving he'd been slouched in his armchair in front of the television. An advertisement for an airline was on.

Jim didn't waste time. 'You took some guy into my room.'

The old man weighed up Jim's mood, was relieved there was no aggression. 'He showed me an ID card.'

'Who was he then?'

'Ach, I can't tell you his name. Police, that's all I know. He wanted you and he wanted to see your room.'

'Did he say why?'

Geordie was losing interest. He pulled the ring on the can while the advertisement was replaced by one for a car. 'I thought you'd know that. He said he'd been before.'

'Well, did he do . . .'

'He didn't do anything up there.'

'Didn't he look in drawers, open cupboards?'

'Didn't touch anything. He told me I could leave him there and I thought not likely, so I stayed. I tell you, Jim, he didn't touch anything.' He took a long drink while Jim was pressing him for more. Then he said: 'Go down the nick if you want to know. What have you got up there, anyway? Crown jewels?'

Jim left him tipping the can again. The advertisements had ended and the programme was resuming. Upstairs Jim lifted the file of cuttings from beneath sweaters in a drawer.

He dumped the Ford in a car park ten minutes' walk from the hotel, the folder locked in the boot. The receptionist greeted him with an ingratiating smile. There were several telephone messages for James B. Orlando but none that needed attention late at night. He crossed the empty foyer to the lift.

When the heavy door of his suite closed behind him, he pulled off shoes and socks and walked over the springy carpet, liking the way the pile stroked his skin. One hand loosened his tie as he poured a measure of whisky. He frittered time looking at the two oil paintings in the room, then filled the onyx whirlpool bath.

It conjured California, this sort of opulence. That girl, Glenda, who'd had the beach-house out at Santa Monica . . . The evening they'd drunk champagne in her jacuzzi on the patio as the sun was setting over the Pacific . . . The headiness of it all, the leap from bumming on the beaches to Glenda's superior place in the sun . . . Those first unbelievable days when everything went right . . . He was the best thing in her life, for days and days, until the phone call and her husband heading west from Washington. No matter, it was a big country, there were women coast to coast, no need to hang around and be pointed out by the elegant set as the pretty boy Glenda picked up on the beach and shook off just before her husband returned. Jim hadn't waited, he'd sneaked away in the night leaving nothing of himself except a faint impression on her pillow.

He'd hitched a ride south, believing he could do what he liked, be what he liked, go where he liked. Freedom was a flavour in the mind. He was going to make up his own life in his own way, never mind the dispirited, demoralized, downright scared folks in pitchfork country. What did they know?

So he'd joined the lowlifes on the Greyhound, hopping, eight hours at a slot, across the country, drowsing in unquiet motels, homing in on art deco bus stations and gliding on east or north or south. Once, he took up with a Vietnam vet but it ended the day the eyes glazed and the plainstown was transformed to battle zone, and bullets ricocheted off McDonald's. Jim jumped a counter, escaped a back way, the crack-crack-crack of the bullets dying as he flew, then the taut silence before the first of the sirens. The Greyhound was ready to run. He sat behind a Bruce Springsteen lookalike and he counted the seconds until the driver shifted his cowboy boots off the dash, let the engine turn over a few times and then rolled the bus and its aura of diesel fumes, towards the bleak beauty of the Great American Emptiness.

Jim lay among the caressing bubbles a long while before he wrapped himself in the hotel's towelling robe, poured a nightcap and went to bed. It wasn't like him to be nostalgic, he cared chiefly about what came next, what he was aiming for and how to get it. Oddly, this night, when he looked over his shoulder at days out of reach, it was with regret. He was twenty-five, those days weren't far back. And their nearness made clear the shaky judgements at the turning points, the tiny mistakes that ultimately forced the big ones.

Next day he cashed Nellie Ramshaw's cheque, warned the hotel staff that if anyone called Ramshaw tried to reach him they were to say he was out. Then he rang Quincey.

The collector was excited to hear from him, nervous too as Jim had allowed him space to fear the offer of the Orlandianum was being retracted, the dream of one day possessing the Orlando collection fading.

'Mr Orlando. I'm so glad you rang. I have the cash and the cutting all ready for you.' He awaited instructions. Jim visualized the brindled head jutting in eagerness.

'I'm off to Paris for the weekend, sir, but I'd sure like to have this settled before I fly out.'

'I could be over there within the hour.'

'No, I'll have my car call by.' He played up the necessity of speed. Twenty minutes later he dispatched the chauffeur, and entertained himself by inventing the scene when the man arrived on Quincey's doorstep, without either James B. Orlando or the Orlandianum. He rang down for coffee, telephoned J. and J. Electrical to say he was taking the day off sick, and he packed Ramshaw's orchid in a padded envelope. With those details taken care of he sat back to await Quincey's frantic phone call.

Quincey kept the chauffeur waiting outside while he rang. Jim soothed him by saying the car would make a return journey with the Orlandianum once payment had been received in full. Quincey, while appreciating the futility of arguing with so eccentric a millionaire as the orchid-loving Orlando, was reluctant to give in. Jim hurried him by claiming he was in a meeting and had to ring off.

Shortly afterwards the hotel let through a call from Nellie Ramshaw.

'I've been trying to reach you for hours,' she cried. 'Well, when are we going to receive your orchid? Have you got it or is it still in Oxford?'

'Sorry, Nellie. Something big came up and I guess I was just so involved that everything else went right by. Sure I have it now, all wrapped up and ready for delivery. I'll send it right over.'

She fussed about the arrangements.

He said: 'No problem, I'll be around until evening. Call me and let me know you're happy with the specimen. Your cheque is right here in front of me and it won't be going near a bank until I get that call. OK?'

Reassured, she rang off. She expected everything to be resolved within the hour. And so, in a quite different fashion, did Jim.

Before noon the chauffeur brought him Quincey's cash, a raggedly wrapped bundle that Jim carried into the bedroom to count before giving the hotel messenger the envelope containing the Ramshaw plant and asking that the chauffeur take it to Quincey. While the chauffeur was away, he hired a taxi and directed the driver to deliver a package, containing the Quincey plant, to Ramshaw's address.

Jim shopped, charging store cards up near the limit. Messages were waiting when he returned to base: call Quincey, call Miss Ramshaw. He rang Nellie and ran through a repertoire of reaction to her news that the specimen she'd received wasn't what he'd promised her. But she fell for his story that the package had been crossed with one destined for another buyer.

'Leave it to me, Nellie,' he said. 'I'll get right on to the guy and we'll have this thing put straight. Expect a call tomorrow before I fly out to Paris.'

He tossed up what to do about Quincey. Tempting to stay mum and pretend to be already in Paris, but the hotel staff might be lax again. Quincey was in no position to go to the police, yet a telephone call would buy Jim another day or two. Jim made the call.

Quincey was ironic, swallowing the story of a mix-up and cursing himself for not insisting on seeing the Orlandianum before handing over his money. He revealed no doubts about Orlando's integrity.

Jim said: 'I had to delay my flight but I'm away to the airport now. I'll see one of my people deals with this.'

'But will that be safe, Mr Orlando?'

'Sure, he won't know what's in the package, only that two have to be swapped over.'

'How long will you be out of town?'

'I should be through in Paris by Monday, but you don't want to wait until my return. We ought to get on to this problem right away, sir.'

Quincey agreed with that.

Being around the hotel was increasingly tricky. Quincey or the Ramshaws could have a crisis of suspicion and arrive to demand their money. Jim went out. He ate in a famously expensive restaurant, there were things he wanted to enjoy before he gave up the Orlando role.

An heiress's party wasn't one of them but when he walked into the hotel foyer late that evening he saw two police detectives. Instead of passing them to reach the lifts, he turned towards the stairs. On the first floor he side-stepped into a birthday ball.

If there had been security on the door earlier, it had given up. No one challenged his right to the champagne or to ask a polka-dotted girl to dance. He was camouflaged among revellers.

The girl was mildly drunk and intended to be more so

before the night ended. But she danced well and that's all he required of her. That plus information. She gushed it without noticing she'd been asked. The birthday girl, she said, was Lucinda something. Lucinda's boyfriend was Nicholas who was the youngest son of the Duke of Somewhere, the frightfully amusing young fellow spraying champagne around was Wendy . . .

'Wendy?' He blurted disbelief. He shouldn't have.

Polka Dots flattened the frills of her low bodice against his shirt front. 'You know, Timmie's cousin. The Honourable Wendover St Clare.' She spoke the name in a jokey upper-crust nasal drawl. The dance carried her away and when she swayed nearer again she continued: 'Why do Americans find British titles so hard? Inverted snobbery, do you think?' Before he could answer her teasing she said: 'Camilla should give you lessons, you're her responsibility after all.'

Jim trawled the room for a Camilla. He asked, 'You know her well, do you?'

'Oh, from so high.' She held a hand down beside her, the height of a four-year-old's head. And then, at the next convenient moment to speak: '*Such* bad luck, but it's good you could come anyway. Lucinda was mad for her to come over, but you know what Camilla's like.'

He chuckled. 'Oh, yes.'

Polka Dots paid it out, unaware that she tantalized and muddled, until he had a fair picture that he was mistaken for one of Camilla's American set, garnered during her spell in Washington, and that Camilla was detained by tragedy in France. He saw no reason to demur, it was entertaining to have someone do the inventing for him.

In a while there was a flurry of balloons and 'Wendy' pulled the cork of some expensive champagne that he wasted on a squealing mêlée of designer dresses. Afterwards there were cars to a nightclub.

Jim travelled with the Polka Dots party. In the car he sat close to her but once in the night club he put a circumspect distance between them. Convinced he was legitimately one of her crowd, the girl had ensured his acceptance. Someone bought him a drink. In a while someone else included him in a group going next door to a gaming club.

The tension, the clatter of chips and the blur of the wheels, kicked on the adrenaline. He wore the tight, narrowly focused expression of the man who's serious about playing, winning, and occasionally losing. Jim took a couple of hundred pounds off a young man who'd been at the birthday party. Their eyes met, the all-knowing, uncommunicative eyes of gamblers.

Jim had once known those eyes well, had wasted nights and cash in pursuit of the big thrill. It was elusive. A win that was big enough one evening was too small for it ever after. Wins had to increase or there was no thrill. He'd found out, escaped in time. This night he was in no danger. He'd come in on a winning streak but lacked interest to ride his luck. Perhaps it was because he wasn't staking himself, he was playing with Quincey's money and old man Ramshaw's money. Or perhaps it was because there was a better game in the nightclub, one with higher stakes and immeasurable risks. He went back.

A woman had taken his seat among the Polka Dots crowd. He hadn't seen her before. He'd have remembered those midnight eyes, the kind of hair that could sell shampoo.

She had a cheeky smile. 'Hello, I've pinched your drink while you've been away.'

He paid for more drinks and drew up a chair. 'Jane Logan,' she said. 'Jilly says you absolutely saved her life at Lucinda's party.'

'I'm James Rush. We danced, I don't recall the life-saving.'

'She was on the run from a lover whose love is destined to go unrequited. Or, to put it another way, I gather he was drunk and she preferred to dance with a man who wasn't.' The smile hadn't gone away, it lingered in the warmth of her eyes, a curve of her lips.

'I didn't see you there, Jane.'

'No, I went to a dinner instead. Fearfully dull but a duty not to be ducked. My treat was to come on here and catch the gossip. Do you have any for me?'

'Not a scrap.'

'Nothing new on Camilla? Jilly says you . . .'

She was interrupted by a woman bounding across from the next table with tittle-tattle that demanded to be whispered deliciously in her ear.

Jim left early, sliding out unobserved and leaving each knot of friends to assume he was with one of the others. Rich, assured, they'd taken him at polka dot Jilly's valuation and he'd dodged saying where he was staying. He cut through streets, sleepy but believing it safer to make for Willesden. At the entrance to the car park he changed his mind, gambled on the hotel.

No policemen were in evidence, no embarrassed or questioning glances from the hotel staff. He seemed safe. He slept.

The telephone rang three times before it roused him. Daylight was sidling around the curtains and sparrows were squabbling on his window sill. Just on eight, early for a call and only two people might be ringing: Quincey or Nellie Ramshaw.

He wrenched at the receiver, angry.

A clerk said: 'Good morning Mr Orlando, I have a Miss Ramshaw on the line for you.'

'I don't care if you have the Virgin Mary on the line, you can tell the lady to call again after nine. I thought I'd made it clear I wasn't to be disturbed.' He hadn't but aggression won the point. The man apologized and cut the connection.

Jim stamped into the bathroom, showered. Then he asked them to book him a flight to Paris that day, and left the hotel. He wanted to think, he'd planned to cover himself by biding his time at J. and J. Electrical for a few weeks more, but he was casting around for an alternative.

He ate breakfast in a café-bar and browsed through newspapers. Down page a paragraph jumped out at him. 'A police spokesman said yesterday that a man is being sought in connection with the death of a British Rail manager, Matthew Reynoldes, in Richmond, Surrey, on July 16. Mr Reynoldes was found dead in his car close to the Thames.'

Jim drank froth off his *cappuccino*. Who? How? Why? What

else was there that wasn't in the story, because there'd be something for sure. There always was.

Penny might know but Penny was out of his reach. For a few days anyway. After that he might try her number, say he missed her, hope his approach didn't raise suspicions.

The café was claustrophobic. The smoggy heat in the streets oppressed him. He needed breathing space. For a few seconds he wondered about Paris, although it was too complicated and dangerous to take up an Orlando booking with a Rush passport. From the café callbox he cancelled James B. Orlando's reservation. The pressure increased. He knew he'd have to disappear, for a day or two, maybe three. He used the telephone again, croaked at Eric Shaw about laryngitis.

A plan was forming: pick up the Ford and follow the road to Cambridge, then on to the emptier parts of Norfolk. He craved crop fields, great skies, and unpeopled nothingness. Norfolk was a mystery beyond the trite calendar photographs in the office, but it sprang to mind because of what that woman, Jane Logan, had said in the nightclub. 'There was a Rush when I was at school. She claimed family ties in Norfolk although she'd always lived in New Zealand herself before Benenden.'

'And did she turn out to be the long-lost lady of the manor?'

'Lord no. She was ghastly. The girls hated her.'

The nuances escaped him, the idea of Norfolk clung. He bought a road map and began the trudge to the car park, circling to avoid the vicinity of the hotel. Fifteen minutes later he was passing an amusement arcade. Out of it stepped a short, stocky figure.

'Hello, Jim. Looking for me, boy?'

O'Malley.

O'Malley looked him up and down. The sharp Italian suit, the quality, the damn good looks that O'Malley himself had never enjoyed. O'Malley wrinkled his nose. 'Smells like money, old son.'

'Now listen,' said Jim, calm on the surface. 'I'm in a hurry right now.'

'That right? I reckon you want to talk to me, though. Explain what became of that nice little thing we had going.'

For the hundredth time Jim regretted the folly of boasting to this man, in a room nine by six with a slit of sky. He attempted to walk on but there were passers-by and café tables on the pavement, preventing a decisive move without drawing attention to himself. 'OK, two minutes. But off the street.'

O'Malley retreated into the arcade.

Truant schoolkids were lounging around the machines, feeding cash into slots, mesmerized by the flicker of lights and the beeps and whoops of electronic money-snatching. Jim followed O'Malley to a gap where the machines broke rank around the recess of a door. O'Malley tried to position himself so that Jim was caught in the gap, the trap. Alert, Jim reversed the situation.

O'Malley's face coloured green and blue and red according to the machines beside him. It made his haggard face and gone-to-seed body grotesque. But he knew people and that made him dangerous. They'd talked once. Where they'd met, men talked to anyone. Out of bravado, or despair.

He said: 'Joe Cornelly says he had you in one day, that they're waiting on you.' He was lighting a cigarette, an unclean smell about him, of old tobacco smoke and a jacket overdue at the cleaners. A scruff, but it didn't mean he lacked brains. The sort of people Jim had met in there, mostly they'd been intelligent. They just hadn't got away with it.

Jim said: 'Sure, I saw Cornelly. I told him the time wasn't right.'

'Yeah, well, we reckon it's time it was. See what I mean?'

Jim batted smoke away from his face. 'You can't roll a guy who hasn't quit LA. I'll know when he comes. We'll go into action then.'

O'Malley was shaking his head. 'You and who else, Jim?'

Jim made an open-handed gesture. 'You if you want it. It's a two-guy job, you know that.'

O'Malley's eyes were half-closed, sceptic. 'Yeah, it had better be, Jim. Because if it isn't . . .'

'Why would I want to play around with you, with Cornelly? I want to go on living in this town.'

'You just make sure . . .'

Rattled, Jim snapped: 'We play this one my way or we don't play it at all.' He backed off. 'You can tell Cornelly I said that.'

O'Malley moved after him, a hand going for Jim's sleeve. The machine next to him spewed out cash, the electronic jabber reached painful levels and the kid leaning on the machine continued to slide money down the slot. Jim pulled free.

He expected the tap on the shoulder, the bump into the wall, but O'Malley didn't pursue. Round a corner, Jim quickened to a run. OK, he'd thrown off O'Malley but word would go out that he was around. From any doorway, from any alley, Cornelly's men could snatch him.

He came to a hotel with a lounge where countless people were coming and going, sitting around. He sat around. He grew ashamed of being unsettled by O'Malley, the guy was nobody. Even Cornelly, that small-time villain aping the style of an old-time underworld gang leader, didn't amount to anything. *Christ*, they couldn't invent their own stuff! Oh sure, O'Malley had talked once about a racket he was in, but it wasn't class, it wasn't clever. That's why he'd battened on when Jim, swapping dreams, had dropped the word about the rich Californian who could be taken quite painlessly for thousands. Painlessly. Ah, yes. That's what made him edgy about O'Malley and his kind. They didn't savour the elegance of doing things painlessly.

Because he was ashamed of being nervous of O'Malley, and because he hated him for being a reminder of unfair and pitiless weeks, he wanted to strike back at him. Petty, foolish, but he wanted to do it and he knew how. So Jim sent for his limousine and gave directions for a hotel in Kent, one advertised in leaflets in the foyer where he sat.

Once there he warned the chauffeur he'd be in a meeting for several hours and tipped him with the price of a lunch near by. The man walked away. Jim found a route through the hotel, down an internal staircase to the car park and started up the limousine. The chauffeur had left his cap on the front seat. As he was leaving the town, Jim put it on.

At the village of Appleton he pulled in to a garage. A young man wiping oily hands down dungarees came out of the workshop ready to wield the petrol pump. Jim said: 'O'Malley sent me. I have to get directions to the farm.'

The man's eyes swept the length of the car. He whistled in appreciation. 'I'll put a gallon in.' The pump swung on a bracket across the pavement. When he'd finished he stood between Jim and any onlookers from the shop over the street. 'Make out you're giving me money for the petrol.'

'Sure.'

They mimed. The man said: 'You go a mile out of the village and take a steep left just after you see a sign for free-range eggs. The track takes you into the farmyard. Drive straight into the barn.'

Jim restarted the engine. The man said: 'Any questions and you buy a box of eggs. Got it?' Then: 'I'll phone up, say you're on your way.'

There was a reception committee in the barn: three men and a woman in jeans and a red blouse. An Alsatian dog, too. Jim got out of the car. 'O'Malley's idea,' he said.

A thick-necked older man nodded. 'The lad in the village rang.'

The other men were taking in the car, not Jim's introduction. The woman said: 'I love that hat.'

Jim took it off. 'Lady, it's yours.' He tossed it to her. The dog leaped for it, but she caught it anyway.

One of the other men asked: 'What do you want?'

O'Malley had talked well and Jim said: 'A third now, and a lift back the other side of town.' He saw no advantage in being greedy, he didn't have the time to haggle.

The oldest man pulled a face. 'It's on the high side. We don't do many of these.'

'I guess you don't get offered many,' said Jim. 'Am I on, or am I taking it down the line?'

The atmosphere told him they were keen, had been from the moment they'd got the telephone call to tell them what was on its way. A third of the retail price was cheap and they all knew it. 'Wait here,' said the third man. He strolled away, hands in trouser pockets, the dog sniffing at his heels.

Jim looked around. Massive beamed roof, plenty of space. He calculated how many cars could be hidden in there, hidden while they were stripped of identification, prepared for shipment and resale.

The man brought fat rolls of cash. Jim counted it out, roughly, on the bonnet of the car. He didn't fear being tricked because they owed loyalty to O'Malley. The sum was correct. He put it in a plastic carrier bag the woman fetched him from her own car in the yard.

'All right, then,' said the man who'd fetched the money. 'Let's head for town.'

Jim said: 'She can do it.' He didn't want to chance pre-arranged villainy. They'd be less likely to set something up if the woman was in the car, and the risk that she'd attack him herself was negligible.

The man objected but the woman plucked keys from her pockets and led Jim to her car. They didn't have much to say on the journey.

'That hat,' he said at one point. 'You ought to lose it.'

'I know. It'll go in the farm boiler tonight.'

They drew close to the hotel and she dropped him off. He entered by a side door and sat in the coffee shop, posing as a man waiting for someone who had let him down. When enough time had elapsed he called up the chauffeur and said he wanted to leave, he had to catch a Paris plane from Gatwick.

While the chauffeur panicked about the missing car and called his office and chased after hotel staff who might have noticed the thief at work, Jim busied himself on the telephone confirming the impression that he was due on urgent business in Paris. He ordered alternative transport to the airport.

At the terminal he paid off the taxi, walked inside, drank coffee, walked out again and hired another cab. He asked the driver to take him to a block of flats in London. It was fifty yards from the car park where his Ford was hidden.

What Jim had said to O'Malley was true: he wanted to go on living in London. The city had the kind of buzz that fed him what he needed. London held out possibilities that Chicago hadn't. He'd failed to make the right moves in San Francisco and he'd quit New York while he was winning. London, he sensed, had been the goal all along. There were things to be grasped, a way of life to be lived. He could make it in a way he couldn't in the States.

And yet he recognized fantasy when he encountered it. His life rested on fantasy, always had done, on the daydream that if he could only gain this, just get away with that, there was a good time to be had, and an end to manipulation, to striving.

The Orlando hoax had provided money, his revenge on O'Malley had paid a bonus, and he was ready to make a break. All that curbed him was the unfortunate business of Matthew Reynoldes's death. Jim dared not make one of his inspired split-second decisions about that, instinct cautioned that he was going to have to do what he dreaded most. He was going to have to sit it out.

Five

Stefan came out of his room as Jim unlocked the attic door. 'Is that you, Jim?'

'Come on up.' Jim hid the cash before Stefan reached the landing. Stefan hovered and Jim said: 'Come in.'

The shirt had escaped entirely from Stefan's waistband. He scrubbed lank hair back from his face. He was more ill-kempt and pinched than ever.

'Any visitors?' Jim inquired, ready for reports of Geordie allowing Boulter and his CID colleagues free rein in his absence.

'No,' said Stefan, going to the window. An InterCity 125 was mourning below, normal livery not the mysterious one with the white roof. 'I knew a boy whose dad bought him a huge train set. They had it spread out in a special room in their house. When you looked down on it, it was nearly like looking down on this.'

Jim grunted. The story was over-familiar. 'I'll bet that boy never let anyone else play with it.'

Stefan was surprised at this perception. 'No, he didn't. Sometimes he'd let other children go and watch. And you'd really want to pull those levers and make the engines do things, but he wouldn't let you.'

'No, I'm sure he wouldn't.'

'And one day one of the kids, Brian he was called, well this Brian he got mad and he pushed him away and grabbed at the control box. And there was a fight. They were all stopped going there after that. Except for me, I used to go sometimes.'

Jim made coffee, handed him a mug. Stefan asked: 'Where've you been then, Jim?'

'Around.' He stirred his coffee. 'I'll be away tomorrow night, maybe the one after. There's a guy in the West Country offering me a job. I thought I'd go down and take a look at it.'

'Paddington,' said Stefan. 'You'll want to go to Paddington to get a train to the West Country.'

Side by side they considered the perpetual motion of the giant train set. After a few unbroken minutes Jim laughed. 'There ought to be a great big control box somewhere, I mean one we could get our hands on. We could throw the switch, bring the whole damn thing to a halt. We could fling it into reverse, have the trains go back where they'd come from.'

'Yes,' said Stefan, uncertain.

'And then we could set them off again, only they wouldn't go the way they'd gone before. We'd have seen the future, so we'd change the directions. Second thoughts.'

Stefan was frowning. 'Why?'

Jim turned to the sink, tipped away the rest of his coffee. He sighed. 'Just an idea.'

There were two things he needed to hide: the file of newspaper clippings and a lot of money. The attic had no fireplace and he didn't want to cross Geordie by lighting a bonfire in the back garden. Concealing the file in a plastic dustbin liner, he added an armful of old papers from the pile in the lobby. The theory was that a local charity collected them for recycling. The truth was that they didn't turn up for three months on end and the lobby was given over to yellowing paper. Jim carried the bulging bin liner to the Ford in a nearby street. Then, while Stefan was out of the house Jim entered his room, shifted the bed, pulled back the carpet, prised up a floorboard and concealed the money.

He drove out of London. Passing through a suburb where dustbinmen were at work, he placed his bin bag beside a pile awaiting collection.

In East Anglia the day was yellow and blue and airy. Churches buttressed the sky, reaping machines crawled from farm to farm changing the face of the land, and banks and hedges were snagged with gold. Rushwood lay at the end of a lane marked 'No Through Road'.

Rushwood, Norfolk. (See also Rushwode.) Population: four. The first el. is OE risc, rysc 'rush', partly riscen adj. 'rushy'. The second el. is OE wudu wood. Possibly 'the wood by the rushy place', although some authorities suggest the first el. might be OE hrif 'womb'. The Church of St Andrew has a typically East Anglian roof, dated 1502, spanning almost 30ft and rich with carved angels. The chancel arch is Norman and there is an Anglo-Saxon window. The manor house dates from the thirteenth century but was much altered in the fifteenth.

Jim jiggled the iron loop on the studded door. Locked. He circled the church, taking in the names on the gravestones. No Rushwodes or Rushwyndes or Rushwoods, but he anticipated them recorded in brassy splendour inside.

The manor house, the only other building, gave the impression of having staggered into position and stayed there by willpower. There wasn't a horizontal or a vertical to be found.

No one answered when he rang the doorbell. He studied the jumbled roofline, the glittery windows. A woman came round the end of the house.

'We use the other door,' she said, in the gentle burr of Norfolk. Elderly ankles bulged over sensible shoes.

'Excuse me, I . . .'

'And there's no one here.'

Jim said he'd hoped for a key to the church.

The woman swatted at a bee drunk on summer. 'Are you on your own?'

'Yes.'

'There isn't much in there, you know.'

'My family came from these parts. I'd be interested to see.'

She decided she liked the look of him. 'Wait there. I'll be back in a minute.'

On their way to the church she eyed his car and he could have sworn she was memorizing the number plate. She said: 'There was a theft three years ago. They took a stone figure.

You wouldn't think that sort of thing had much value, but apparently there's a market. We've locked up ever since.'

She fiddled the iron key with the fancy handle into the lock. 'There.'

When his eyes adjusted from sunlight, the host of angels flew above shadowy stone. Rushwoods – and Rushwynds and Rushwodes – lay in marble and were lettered in brass, they gleamed in a window. His Aunt Maria's admiral was recorded as going down with his ship. Others had gone up: in the Church of England or by making good marriages. Daughters had linked themselves to Sir This and the Duke of That. Maria had talked about connections and that was the word. The Rushwoods were well connected.

The woman who'd opened up was dragging weeds from around a grave. 'All done?' She straightened. 'Wasn't much to see, was there? I did warn you.'

He said it was a charming church. 'I guess the house isn't on the itinerary too?'

'I should think not. Mrs Hamptonbury wouldn't care for that.'

'That's a real shame. It looks just perfect from the outside.' But there was never a serious chance of her letting him over the threshold. She said goodbye and that she was glad he'd enjoyed the church.

In a pub he learned that an industrialist called Hamptonbury had bought the house in the 1970s and his widow lived there with a housekeeper; that the property had passed out of the hands of Rushwoods when Queen Victoria was on the throne; and what remained of the family was female and no longer in the county. His grasp of English aristocracy was weak but he understood that for modern Rushwoods he'd have to search among foreign capitals. Norfolk could show him some of the stations on their progress, the stately homes.

His face in the pool, illusion and reality. He stretched out a hand and its double reached for him. Fingers strained but dared not meet. Where would it go, this parallel self, what would become of it when he moved away? He fancied crossing the barrier of the water's skin, experiencing that truth.

Mundane answers were for people who accepted plain truths. The pool butted fact and fantasy, or perhaps they were congruent realities. Tentative, his fingers eased forward a fraction. Testing. He wanted to become the other one, saw escape in the film of the pool.

The face was handsome. Fine features, blue eyes, a firm chin, and fair hair falling over his forehead. The clothes were perfect and the outheld hand strong and slim. He admired his physical appearance as he might the lines of a sleek car. The effect was one of relaxed self-confidence. A smile lit the colour of his eyes, his lips parted to allow the narrow white edge of teeth. His hand moved too. He saw that it had ceased to strain, that it had become a gesture of supplication.

Jim held the pose, studying his smile as it faded. He was proud of his body and proud that it didn't rule him. Sexual desire was neither paramount nor frequent. He disappointed by rejection more often than he was disappointed. Other people's expectations of him were wrong: they attributed attitudes and appetites that weren't his. They invented him, ignoring evidence and cultivating stereotypes. People always invent other people, cramming them willy-nilly into tidy slots until all family, friends and acquaintances appear to make up a standard cast of personalities. Because no one can truly know anyone else, invention becomes necessity.

Jim and the man in the pool brushed hair back from foreheads. The upward sweep of the arm was an involuntary beckoning. A potential world lay before him, to be attained in a moment of magic or shattered as a finger touched water. He savoured the dilemma, resting hands on the stone rim, keeping the fantastic opportunity alive.

Always he'd invented himself, deliberately, over and over. He broke free of convention and restraint and he remade himself. So many guises before that streetwise New York guy making out until the heat, the flight. Over and over, the posing, the slip and the mask sliding. Retreat. Restart. Recreate. Make it new and make it better. One day, make it last.

A sparrow skipped along the stone, shimmered the water with its beak. Jim walked to the house, although he knew the door was shut against visitors and he would see no more than linings of thick curtains and wooden shutters behind glass.

The land belonged to King Harold and after the Conquest William gave it to Herbert de Losinga, the Bishop of Norwich and builder of Norwich cathedral. The present house was completed in 1628 and altered from 1767–79. The red cliff of its façade is lightened with bay windows topped with ogees, and the roof is capped by a turret with an open-topped lantern. The house has always been rich if not regal. Among its greatest treasures are a magnificent staircase and the Long Gallery with its carved plaster ceiling.

A flowered way led to a bridge. Swans on the lake, moorhens scuttling among reeds, and a dutiful heron. Along came the grey shadows of little fishes. Jim watched the heron. A stab, a swallow and on guard. A neat clean end and a fresh beginning. He took a short cut to the gate, abandoned the seventeenth century and drove to the coast.

There was a sly curl to Eric Shaw's mouth, a glint of malice in his eye. Jim couldn't help himself.

'What do you mean, Eric?'

'Work it out, Jim. You think you're sharper than the rest of us.' He turned to the telephone, tapped out a number. Jim shot an exasperated look towards the ceiling. He pictured himself plucking the receiver out of Shaw's hand, trapping him in the space between the desk and the wall, threatening him until he spilled it out. Pictured it, and identified it as a temptation to be resisted. He flung out of the office.

An old man was buying a three-pin plug. A woman with a shopping trolley was staring through the window at a cheap offer for microwave ovens. Television screens blinked along one wall of the shop. Jim lounged against a washing machine and feigned watching an Australian soap, probably *Neighbours*, he wasn't certain.

He could work out several things that might have happened, all of them to be dreaded in differing degrees. Detective Sergeant Boulter might have pursued his inquiries about Jim's whereabouts on the Tuesday and two Thursdays when crimes were committed on his patch; or the Hodgeses might have decided they wanted their satellite dish moved; or Nellie Ramshaw might have gone to the police with a description of the man who'd passed himself off as James B. Orlando; or the Richmond police might have learned that a fair-haired young man had been seen getting into Matthew Reynoldes's car and that a similar but bedraggled man had been getting into a J. and J. van hours later; or . . .

The soap ended. One of the office vans flashed by the window. Jim sauntered into the yard. The van was turning in. He stood by the driver's door.

'Hi, Alex.'

Alex flashed a grin. 'You still here? Eric's giving me all the plum jobs today, is he?' He tried to open the door but Jim didn't budge.

Jim said: 'Thought you might know what's going on around here. Eric's being a mite mysterious.'

'Well, you know Eric. He's just a . . .' His second attempt to get out failed. He registered the set of Jim's jaw. 'Oh, look. Don't get this wrong, Jim. I didn't say it was to do with you. Eric made up his own mind about that, just jumped straight to it.'

'Oh yes?'

'Yes. I was going to warn you, honest, I was.'

'But?'

'But he sent me out, didn't he? All the way over to Kew.'

'I don't care where you went, Alex. Just tell me what you've done.'

Alex was struggling with the door. 'Will you let me out of this thing?'

'Tell me.'

Alex flinched. He'd heard that tone of voice once before. 'Jim, please. It's only Eric, it doesn't matter.'

Jim had his hands on the edge of the opened window and held it firm when Alex tried to close it. 'What did you do, Alex?'

Alex collapsed then, let go of the door and ran fingers through his hair. 'Jim, it wasn't like that. I didn't know Eric would put it on you. I mean, I didn't think he'd ever find out about it.'

Jim brought a fist down on the roof of the van. 'For Christ's sake, Alex!'

The youth's face went white, then there were deepening red spots on his cheekbones. 'It was your bloody idea,' he shouted.

Jim groaned, leaning his forehead against the scorching metal of the van. 'You didn't, Alex. Oh God, you *didn't*.'

'You said it would wind Eric up. And it was brilliant, Jim. *I'd* never have thought of it.' He blustered on until Jim sighed and moved away from the door. Alex got out. Tentative, he asked: 'What are we going to do, then?'

'*We*?'

'Yeah, I know. I did it, not you. But . . .'

'But you've made sure we're both in the shit. Right?'

Alex rubbed sweat from his face. His colour was coming back. He shrugged, resignation rather than nonchalance.

Jim asked him: 'Can you get the stuff back? Any of it?'

'Are you serious?' It's screwed on to houses all over London.'

'Satellite stuff, nothing else?'

'Only that stuff.'

'Well, there is a way but it won't be easy.'

'Jim, anything that will stop Eric getting the law in is all right by me.'

'I have to think. Don't say anything yet, let it ride.'

'OK. Jim, I . . . er . . .'

'Sure. You're sorry.'

Alex looked across at the office window. 'I'd better get in there.'

'Right. If anybody asks, I've gone to the newsagent's.' He took several steps before he looked back. Alex was approaching the office door but without his usual swagger.

Jim browsed, fingering magazines. There was nothing specific he wanted, he was in hiding until his temper subsided and he recovered his nerve. The thought racketed around in his brain that stupid, reckless Alex had made the blunder that undermined everything, that his fate rested in the hands of that dolt.

Jim had lied when he'd told Alex there was a way to avert trouble. It wasn't even bravado, just a way of staving off the moment when Alex tried something of his own invention and, inevitably, exacerbated the situation.

He was weighing up whether to quit J. and J. and leave Eric Shaw and the police to mop up their little problem any way they chose, or whether to stay and brave it out, letting Alex carry the blame. There was risk either way. If he stayed the Acton police would probably question him, and perhaps it would lead to a further session with Detective Sergeant Boulter. All that would be uncomfortable but if he left his job under suspicion more serious inquiries would ensue. Suppose they issued a description of him as a man wanted in connection with the Acton theft? How soon before it clicked that the description tallied with 'Orlando'? And what if the Richmond police had a witness who'd described the man with Matthew Reynoldes the evening he died?

The shopkeeper came to tidy the shelves and Jim suffered a pang of conscience and bought a copy of *Tatler*. He walked a few yards along the main street to J. and J. There were no customers in the shop, no buffers against trouble. Eric Shaw and Alex were in the office. Their silence was unpleasant. Jim checked the job list. There was a job in Acton. He lifted the van keys off the hook and went out. Still nobody spoke.

The customer was an inadequate man with a treacherous dog. Jim negotiated for the creature to be kept indoors while he worked outside but, when he wanted to come down the ladder into the front garden, the dog was growling at the bottom. It dislodged the ladder which slipped sideways, dragging against the brick wall under the eaves. Jim got a hand on the guttering and made a futile effort to straighten the ladder.

The dog leaped again, nudging it further off true. Jim shouted for the owner. The edge of the guttering was rough beneath his hand. Shouting excited the dog which began barking. Jim imagined the owner dashing out of the door and rescuing him, but the scene never became reality.

Instead, the frenzied dog hurled itself at the lower rungs and Jim felt the ladder twist away. His feet swung with it, one hand flailed and the other was wrenched free of the guttering. For an instant he was poised high on a ladder that was deciding which way to plunge. And then it was gone and he was following it earthwards, at sickening speed yet with time to visualize injuries inflicted by impact with its metal frame.

Wild with its success, the dog rushed forward, snapping at the air. The dog broke the fall. Jim's first breath-sucking contact wasn't with cruel rungs or the hardness of parched lawn but with the overweight furry body of the dog. Construing this as attack, the animal savaged him as he lay there, its breath terrible in his face and its teeth grinding into his right shoulder. He raised a hand to fend it off and knew in the instant of raising it that teeth would crunch on knuckles. He was too engaged to feel pain. He smashed out with his free hand, cracking into the dog's skull hard enough to make it falter but inadequate to curb its fury.

He was scrabbling to get up but the dog was above him, knocking him on to his back, his legs bent beneath him and his bloodied hands seeking to protect his throat. He saw nothing but the redness within his eyelids, felt visceral terror.

And then it ended. The dog withdrew. There were voices in the garden. The snarling receded as the animal was dragged away. Jim lifted his hands and looked up into the face of a woman. He saw a very anxious face framed with mousy hair. And a hat. She was wearing a hat. She knelt down, a glimpse of dark-stockinged knee beneath a dark skirt.

'Are you all right?' She had an unmusical Cockney voice. It was the most beautiful thing he'd ever heard.

He tried to nod, to answer, but the pain had arrived. He let out his breath in anguish.

Her consoling hand touched his arm. 'You're lucky we came past.'

Lucky. To be on the run from the police and rescued by a policewoman. Jim groaned and shut his eyes.

Her colleague, the hero who'd used his truncheon to cow the dog, hurried from the house where the owner had been roused and ordered to lock up the monster. Together the police checked for the worst kinds of injury. Can you move this? Does that hurt? And when there were no obviously broken bones they offered a ride to the hospital rather than a wait for an ambulance. He let them settle him into the back seat, where he bled all the way, soaking through pads that were meant to staunch.

The woman drove. The man talked over his shoulder, ironic. 'Bet you thought you had a nice quiet kind of job.'

Jim rose to the occasion with wryness. 'I guess I just quit.'

The woman said: 'We came round the corner and the ladder caught my eye. Just standing there, sort of upright and you parting company with the top of it.'

At the hospital there was cleaning and stitching and injecting. Paperwork too, and a plastic beaker of tea. The policewoman explained how he could lodge a complaint against the owner of the dog, although her colleague added his own observation that as the incident had happened on private property and not in a public place the police wouldn't handle it. Jim put on a show of polite attention and gratitude. The gratitude was genuine but he meant to let the owner go unpunished.

When the patrol car had left and the hospital had finished with him, he called Eric Shaw to say he'd fallen. Shaw seized this opportunity for comment on Jim's unsuitability to work on installations for so noble a firm as J. and J.

Jim cut through it. 'Don't expect me in for a few days, Eric.'

Shaw retorted that taking time off was becoming a habit. Jim didn't hear him out, he hung up.

The damage was slight. There'd been blood and there'd be soreness but nothing to keep him off work unless he wanted an excuse. He did.

The house in Tubbs Road was empty. He stood in front of his mirror. Traces of blood marked his face although it hadn't been cut, the blood had come from his hand. Jim showered, swallowed painkillers and lay down.

The room depressed him with its jumbled cast-offs: the lampshade with the forget-me-nots, the chipped Formica table, the orange and green rug that tiptoed up the room instead of stretching out beside the bed. He closed his eyes to it, conjured up the comforts of James B. Orlando's hotel suite.

But the trains invaded and the daydream changed its style to rustic, and the room in the daydream shrank and took on a tipsy ceiling and a white-framed casement that showed a flare of high corn in golden fields. The essence of those fields was wafted to him in a blend of imagination and memory. Summer, a vicious one, and the stillness of the farm bedroom hummed inside his head. Gradually the hum changed into something else, a vehicle approaching. The sound died. A voice called. Lethargic, he went down the wooden stairs and towards the open door. The sun tore into him as he came out on the step. He shaded his eyes with a browned hand . . .

In Tubbs Road, Willesden, London, the front door thudded and the house reverberated. Stefan had returned. If it had been Geordie there would have been an old man's shuffling along the hall and the sound of another door. Because there was nothing, Jim knew it was Stefan moving catlike up to his first-floor room. Jim reached out a hand and checked that his own door was locked. He hated that, much preferred it wide, but Stefan was a burden he didn't want to carry right now.

He lay and thought about Stefan, an unoriginal chain of thoughts that led from his personality to his illness to his empty days. Jim didn't know what he did with his days, apart from the visits to social services offices and periods of train spotting. Jim filled the gaps with speculation, about the people he came into contact with, about whether he'd discovered sex.

He slept until late evening, waking refreshed and restless, determined not to waste time. While Stefan's television chattered, Jim slipped out of the house.

The gaming club admitted him, he began to lose and not to mind. Not minding was potentially dangerous. Players who never caught the bug were the ones appalled by losing. He wasn't interested in the game, but in the other players.

He wanted to learn who else didn't mind losing, who'd go for high stakes and damn the consequences.

There were two possibilities: A Middle Eastern man of around forty and an Englishman with receding hair although no older than his middle twenties. Jim studied their play, then concentrated on his own and won back some of what he'd parted with earlier. He intended to leave the table for a while, buy a drink at the bar, but the croupier misinterpreted and included him in the next game. He stayed on, to win and to lose. Then he went next door to the nightclub. A couple of people he'd met on his first visit invited him to join them. He'd tapped into something invaluable. Because of an assumption that he knew a woman called Camilla, everyone in her sphere deemed it reasonable to treat him as a friend. No more insinuating himself, justifying his presence, no more effort. Skilled as he was at contriving the incident that led to contact, at nurturing contact into trust, he fully appreciated a milieu where none of that was required.

The couple's friends arrived. Jim's acquaintance expanded. A newcomer asked: 'No one else here yet?'

'I think Jo-Jo's next door,' said a woman. 'Told me he was feeling lucky today.'

A man called Rory asked Jim: 'Do you play, James?'

'A little, I guess. Now and then.'

'Come on, then. Let's see how it looks tonight.' Rory rose.

'Oh, I . . .'

'Yes, come on.'

Jim feigned reluctance but went with him. Rory whispered, 'We'll watch Jo-Jo for a minute or two.'

The man he meant was the young Englishman with the thinning hair. He was winning, not hugely. Rory suggested he and Jim join the game.

This pleased Jim because he'd had to leave the table rather than let it appear that a duel might be developing between himself and the man he now knew as Jo-Jo. In the meantime the Middle Eastern man had dropped out and all the other players had changed. Returning in Rory's company disguised his interest.

Jo-Jo acknowledged their arrival with a brief word to Rory,

then concentrated again. Rory was clumsy and lost, although he recovered a few pounds here and there. Jo-Jo was down overall. Although Jim tried to match their play, he had a good win, in excess of two thousand pounds, and decided he'd better attempt to give some of it back before quitting.

He was doing this when a woman came to stand behind Jo-Jo. Jane Logan, the one who'd talked about gossip and Norfolk. She was smiling her half-smile, weaving through the knots of onlookers. Jim felt her close to him, then she floated away and he saw her near Rory. Between games she draped an arm across Rory's shoulders and murmured. He pushed back his chair, signalling Jim to go with them. For Jim the timing was bad, but he trailed out anyway. Jo-Jo stayed.

Jane wanted them to meet some other friends, that's what she said. There were introductions, drinks, food was ordered. Jane sat next to Jim. It wasn't apparent how people paired off but he suspected she was unattached. He hadn't seen her with anyone particular the other evening either. He told her charming meretricious anecdotes, told them to her and her companions. There was much laughter.

Laughter carried him a long way. If he could get people to smile, persuade them to laugh, they would do things for him. He was careful not to dominate, to let Rory's stories cap his or to allow Jane the final word with one of her sly jokes. Too soon it ended, Jane's protestations that she had to go home, that she had work in the morning, were unexpected. He'd taken her for one of those refined creatures who squandered their nights in clubs and their mornings in bed, their afternoons counting up their private incomes. *Work?* No, he hadn't been prepared for that.

They left together, Jim pleading an early appointment, and took a taxi. He'd claimed to be using a friend's London flat, thinking that if he named a hotel someone might check. Now he said that Kensington, where Jane lived, wasn't far off his route. She sank back, and began to tell him amusing gossip. But when she paused for his reaction, he said: 'Jane, why did you do it?'

Her face was shadowed, unreadable. 'Why did I do what?'

'Break up the game.'

'Did I?'

'You did.' He laughed. 'You sure as hell did, and I'd love to know what it was all about.'

Jane Logan had a childlike way of touching the rim of her teeth with the tip of her tongue, she did it to give herself time to think. Then she stopped the pretence. 'You're right. I wasn't happy with it.'

'Why not?' If she'd suspected things weren't as he'd wanted them to appear, then the sooner he knew it the better.

She said: 'Basically, you know, I'm a puritan. No, don't mock. I mean it, James.'

But then they both laughed before she could go on: 'There's a teeny bit of me that doesn't like gambling.'

'*Any* gambling?'

'That sort. Risks are fine, life would be deadly without them. I enjoy the thrill of the calculated risk as much as anyone but when I heard Rory and you were in there I thought I would be more comfortable if you weren't.'

He gave a playful tweak to her long loose hair. 'You're not making a whole heap of sense.'

'Well now you've learned the importance of the English hint as a social tool. It saves dreary explanations.'

'Or would, if I were bright enough to pick up the hint.'

'You're bright, James. I have you down as very bright indeed.'

His heart sank. He'd believed he'd been getting away with it, but all along she'd been close, perhaps ahead. 'But not quite bright enough?' His words revealed more of his true emotion than he liked. Regretful. Found out.

She touched his hand, her fingers sliding over the bandage until she brushed his fingertips. Her voice was quieter but retained her normal touch of light-heartedness. 'I didn't want anybody to lose more than he could afford.'

Jim struggled to salvage something from the situation, matching her tone. 'Can I come again if I promise not to strip any of your friends of their inheritances?'

She shook her head, laughing. Then: 'Honestly, Rory's a

bastard. I hate to be disloyal and he's *such* an old friend but he was going to take you for your last cent.'

'Is that so?'

'I've known him do that. And if you think about the way he was playing tonight, during the short time I was there . . . Isn't that what they do – get the other player's confidence, raise the stakes sky high and then go in for the kill?'

He excused her muddled metaphor, her confused theory, and said: 'What about your other friend, Jo-Jo?'

'Oh, Jo-Jo's not like that. In any case he could spend the rest of his life playing – probably will, come to think of it – before he inflicts harm on anybody else.'

Jo-Jo was the one, then. Not the Middle Eastern man and definitely not Rory.

He squeezed her hand. 'Well, I guess I have to thank you for a timely intervention.'

Quickly she said: 'James, this is just between us, all right? I'm feeling pretty disloyal to Rory already. I expect he'd see that I had to do it, but of course he'd never see that I had to explain to you too. James, you do understand, don't you?'

'My lips are sealed. Permanently.' He mocked her with gravity. Then added: 'One loose end to tie up. Why do you say you "had" to do it?'

'Camilla!' she cried. 'God, Camilla would have killed Rory if he'd done it to one of *her* friends.'

He mulled over the evening as he lay in the caressing water of the jacuzzi bath at the hotel. Commonsense dictated that he abandon the Orlando disguise before the orchid collectors and the law came for him, but he didn't want to waste the chance to stay in central London and spend his evenings at the clubs. Jane didn't go every evening, but she'd given him her telephone number and he knew where she worked. She was a publicist for an art gallery.

Hard-headed, practical, he could list the advantages of a relationship with Jane. Not necessarily a love affair, another kind would serve. Yet when he thought about her he thought first of her languorous sexual come-on. She wasn't merely decorative, rich, kind and attracted to him; she was also humorous and high-spirited. Yes, he was willing to take a chance on her.

The thought was his last on falling asleep that night, his first on waking. It brought him a buoyancy he hadn't experienced since the realization that both Quincey and the Ramshaws had fallen for the Orlando trick. The thought nourished his imagination. He daydreamed lavishly.

Breakfast was brought to his room while he was dressing. He wandered barefoot from the bedroom moments later, buttoning a shirt cuff, greedy for the day's first cup of coffee. They always set a dainty table for him, with delicate china, orange juice in a crystal jug, and a jaunty twist to the napkin. And they folded his newspaper just so.

Jim poured the coffee, stood irresolute while he sipped half a cup. He had more stuff to sell to the man who looked like a rabbi. Maybe he'd do that today. Or perhaps leave it for a day or two, maybe today he'd . . .

He deferred decision, sat down and lifted the cover on the serving dish. Rashers, sausages, kidneys . . . It must have been one of the most comprehensive English breakfasts in London. He replaced the cover, unfolded the newspaper. World events didn't concern him, since he'd known Jane the gossip columns had intrigued him. He turned the pages, chasing the half-page of those inconsequential snippets. Before he reached it he saw an item that sent him into ice-cold shock.

James B. Orlando, junior had been killed in a fall from limestone cliffs in Borneo while hunting for one of the world's rarest orchids.

Six lines on one of the foreign news pages. Enough to ruin him. Yet the home news pages would have meant a fist hammering on his door by now, the foreign pages gave him a chance. People always read the home news first.

He was stuffing things into a briefcase and a small bag. With luck nobody at the hotel would read about the accident and it might be weeks before they realized the man in room 239 had skipped. Jim crammed into bags and pockets everything destined for Hampstead Garden Suburb.

He examined the room, ensuring signs of occupation.

American cash was in a drawer, along with underwear. One of the good suits hung in the wardrobe with shoes lined up beneath it. Toiletries were scattered on shelves in the bathroom. Fine. Every indication that he'd gone about his business for the day and would be back before nightfall, or at least within a few days. That pattern of movement had already been established and would appear to be continuing.

He snatched up the briefcase, reached for the other bag, and as he did so the table loomed into view. Jim swore. How the hell could he leave his breakfast untouched? Or the newspaper beside it with the tell-tale paragraph waiting to catch an inquisitive eye?

With impatient movements, he shifted a selection of food from the serving dish and the toast rack on to the plate and then emptied the plate on to the newspaper. At a glance, and that's all it would get, it would seem that he'd eaten a normal meal before leaving. Retrieving a plastic carrier bag from the litterbin, he pushed the newspaper parcel into it. At last he was ready to run.

He used the stairs, went out by a side door and hailed a taxi. 'Waterloo,' he said, the first destination that entered his head. The taxi driver wanted to talk. Jim was off-putting, he had more pressing things to consider than the pot-holed state of the capital's roads.

When he'd paid the man off he walked towards the South Bank Centre, a man hurrying along with all the other hurrying men. Only they were going to work and he was going into hiding. He handed the parcel of cooling breakfast to the first tramp who accosted him, then he headed for a café.

Fingerprints, of course. All over the room. Every kind of personal detail left behind. But would it matter? The police didn't have his fingerprints on file. They'd held him, unfairly, but they'd had no case and the court had turned him loose. Maids would dust and vacuum, eventually the room would be re-let. After half an hour he shrugged it off. A guessing game, that's all it was.

One: When will Nellie Ramshaw and Quincey learn of Orlando's death?

Two: Will they alert the hotel?
Three: How quickly will the charge-card companies and the stores uncover the ruse?

He headed for Hampstead. The old man received him with a repetition of his earlier reserve. They reached an agreement and the man counted out used notes, chanting the figures in an accent that was heavy, central Europe. Then he looked up from beneath unruly brows. 'You don't come any more.' A request, not inquiry.

'Tell me why you say this.'

'I don't know you. I prefer you don't come.'

'OK.' Jim took a step towards the door.

The man spoke again. 'Last time you come you telephone, you say O'Malley, but . . .' His shoulders hunched. 'Who knows O'Malley?'

'OK, OK, I'm not coming again. But we don't have to pretend you don't know O'Malley.'

'Goodbye, Jim.'

Jim stiffened. He relaxed into a laugh. 'You know my name! *Christ*. O'Malley tells me about you, he tells you about me. And you pretend you don't know him. Hey, did he warn you off?'

'I don't want trouble. It's no good for business.'

Jim was going to make a pithy remark about the exact nature of the business but the man spoke first.

'I give you advice, Jim. What use is trouble? You don't need it.'

Jim forgot about the pithy remark. He said, with no trace of humour: 'I can handle O'Malley.'

The man spread his hands. 'Ach. Who takes advice?' He turned away and left Jim to let himself out of the house.

Six

Hers was a negligent love, if indeed it was love. The steamy heat of Glenda's passion at the house in Santa Monica and his fearful fumbling with Rosanna in the barn belonged to a different pursuit. Jane Logan liked to take her time. Much of what passed between them was oblique. He liked that.

She stepped out of the shower wearing a white towel around her wet hair. She was happy, teasing. 'It'll be a super party and I shall flirt with Benjy because I always do. But beware, James, I shall tell everyone you're spoken for.'

Pearls of water ran down her pinkened body. She'd tipped forward and let the towel swing open so that she could rub her hair. Then she swathed herself in a robe and went back into the shower room. He heard a hair-drier start up.

Jim combed his hair in front of a mirror in the bedroom. That would be the worst of living with someone, he thought. Not having free access to mirrors and shower rooms. He slid the comb into his pocket, considered his reflection, then took the comb out and ran it through his hair again.

He liked the idea of a country-house party: fluting voices, outlandish behaviour, absurd nicknames and uncaring excess. Ah, and the delicate tread of meandering feet on ancient oak boards as guests went bed-hopping through the night. He knew the cliché by heart. Who didn't?

Jane had asked the hotel to chill champagne. They'd drunk a glass, then walked on the sandy beach and been drenched in the downpour. When she finished with her hair, and put on her necklace and flowered-silk dress, he poured more.

'You'll love Tessa,' she said between sips. 'Well, not *too* much, if you don't mind. She's a sweetie. And we're being awfully considerate and staying here to give her a clear run with Adam.'

'Adam?' She threw so many names at him, he couldn't bother to keep pace. All her friends seemed the same anyway.

'He's married to Clara. She's Dinny's cousin, did I mention that?'

'As explanations go, this one's opaque.'

She said: 'Simple. Next time Adam will be married to Tessa. Of course, he doesn't know that yet. He and Clara are deeply unsuited and it would be a far, far better thing etc. That's why I passed up my claim on Tessa's spare beds so that she can keep Adam and Clara under her roof.

He reran his mental picture of country-house bed-hopping. It was unclear how Tessa could go hopping into bed with Adam if Clara was already ensconced. On the other hand, maybe Adam could prowl the corridors in search of Tessa. Providing that Clara was a heavy sleeper.

His expression seemed comical, she burst out laughing. 'Oh forget it, James. I'm only warning you off fancying Tessa or taking pity on Adam who's a mite forlorn.'

It was true, what she said. Benjy was a dashing type given to talking about sports cars and skiing and Jane was coquettish. Tessa was loveable and Adam was lamentable. Jim didn't discover which one was Clara.

He was shyly sociable, nagged by the fear that Camilla would be there. The worst that had happened so far was that people murmured sympathy about her undefined predicament in France or asked the occasional question about her adventures in Washington. Jim fudged the American stuff and avoided the French. At Tessa's party a woman's voice rang out with: 'Camilla, *darling!*' and he steeled himself. But the Camilla who was being darlinged was another and danger passed.

Three women sang *a cappella*, saying it was a preview of an act they were going to do for charity, and a wag quipped that it would be more charitable not to. A bored fellow called Rupert scouted the room, gathering rejections from those who were having enormous fun. Jim said yes to him. In a study at the rear of the house he won a fair sum playing backgammon. Jane was congratulatory but once they were on their own, in the car to the hotel, he detected a slight *froideur*.

He asked her: 'Are you mad that I played backgammon instead of watching you play games with Benjy?'

'I'm happy you won.' She snuggled up to him, head on his shoulder. Yet he was convinced something was wrong.

Jane hung up the Do Not Disturb sign on the door of their room and pressed her body against his in the wide bed. She stroked his face, ran her fingers over his chest, down his stomach. She said, faking petulance: 'I wanted to show you off and you went into hiding.'

'OK, next time no backgammon.' It was difficult to concentrate on conversation as she was kneading his flesh.

'I've said we'll go over to Tessa's for lunch tomorrow. OK?'

'Er . . . yes. Sure.'

She also lost interest in conversation as he slid a thigh across her.

Tessa had ordered lunch to be served on the lawn, not left-overs from the party but a separate feast prepared by her kitchen staff. There were six guests plus Tessa and a man with an indeterminate relationship with her. It was this man who asked Jim about Camilla. A pigeon-chested woman called Caroline watched unblinking and waited for his reply.

Jim began by asking: 'Did any of you people get over to Washington while she was there?'

He'd achieved the attention of every one of them, determined to get the subject out of the way and not have each individual peck away at it as time went by. There were noes and shakes of the head. Sarah, a freckled waif reminiscent of the young Mia Farrow, said: 'My sister saw Camilla over there but I was at school.'

'Well, you'll have heard what a hit she made,' said Jim, who'd gathered that much from various remarks. Nods and echoes of agreement, and then he spun them a story about Camilla at a Washington event, knowing how people prefer the sweep of anecdote to listed details. He'd seen Washington, he'd read gossip columns and watched television, he thought he could conjure the world in which Camilla had moved. Throughout the story he was conscious that Caroline's eyes never left him.

The man who started it all asked: 'How did you meet her, James?'

'At a party.' The safe, dull answer.

Then a follow-up from the man: 'What took you to Washington?'

Jim had let them believe his base was Connecticut, when he wasn't in New York. The change of tack was unwelcome. Vague answers would soon be inadequate, he was apparently going to be asked to justify his presence in Camilla's life and in theirs. Still he had no option but to go for the vague answer and hope to delay. 'Oh family things. Politics, money.'

Jane sneezed. 'I'm sorry. Hay fever, I'm afraid.'

Tessa became apologetic about having the table set up under the apple tree. Jane rummaged in her pockets for handkerchiefs and cursed a civilization that could put men on the moon but not help people through an English summer without *this* happening to them. Tessa sent Jim's inquisitor into the house to fetch tissues. Caroline lost interest in Jim.

Jane blew her nose and dabbed at her eyes while Tessa sympathized. Caroline's husband, Simon, a big man with clattering consonants talked to Jim about a boat, said Jim should sail with him one weekend. Jim said he'd like that, but he was uncomfortable, wondering when they might come full circle to Camilla.

Jane drove him to her flat, passed over a bottle of white wine and opener. She rested her weight on the edge of the kitchen table while he pulled the cork. She said: 'You had a rotten time. I'm very cross with them.'

'I enjoyed the backgammon.'

'And I'm particularly angry with Roland. There was no need for him to quiz you.'

'I'd have shunted him off if it had become heavy. Who is the guy, anyway?'

'Tessa's brother, of course. Didn't I tell you that?'

He couldn't recall. So many names and so many faces and

few of them stood out from the blur. He said: 'Tessa and Roland don't seem at all alike. Not in appearance or anything.'

'Ah well, Mummy always says you never quite know with Daffy. That's Tessa's mother.'

They went through to the sitting room, Jane barefoot over the rug – a silky Oriental affair fit to fly away on – to listen to messages on her telephone-answering machine. A friend invited her to supper, another wanted her to make up a party to a nightclub, her sister left a complicated message about their parents' departure on holiday, and then Tessa came on the line.

'Oh do ring, Jane,' she pleaded. 'I absolutely must talk to you.' She didn't sound frantic, she fizzed with a tale to tell. Or, worse, questions.

Jane asked him to stay on but when he said he needed to get back to the flat he was using, she didn't put up a fight. She offered to call a cab.

'No,' he said, 'I'll pick one up on the street.'

She linked her hands behind his neck and drew him into her kiss. 'We'll do something nicer next weekend,' she whispered. 'Keep it free?'

'Sure.'

'I'm being greedy, but if you're not going to be around long then I must grab what I can.'

Heat beat up from stone, traffic swirled dust. London had seen no rain for weeks and the weather showed no sign of breaking. Cabs were scarce but his bag wasn't heavy and he felt like walking, perhaps the whole distance to the car park where he'd left the Ford. As he started across the road, a horn sounded. He leaped back, temper rising. And then he realized that the sports-car driver wasn't remonstrating, she was saying hello.

'Small world, as they say.' She gave that big Penny Reynoldes smile before forcing his attention on her companion. 'You remember Clive, don't you?' He recognized it as Clive's car that Penny was driving.

Jim said hi to Clive and Clive glowered.

Penny mentioned they had been to see someone she was

wheedling for a place at a Kensington crammer. Then: 'Well, see you around.'

'Sure. See you around, Penny.'

She'd looked adorable, golden hair disordered, her skin glowing, a girlish eagerness about her. Her father was believed murdered, her mother was distraught and Penny was in full bloom. But what were the families of murder victims meant to do? Hide indoors with the blinds down or maintain visible anguish until villains were apprehended? At Penny's age life went vigorously on.

Next day he'd telephone her, he thought. There had been encouragement in her smile. Despite her practicality in telling him to keep away, she didn't want to let go.

A taxi dropped a woman and her airline luggage outside a pastel-pink house with a geranium on the step. Jim gave up walking and rode to the car park. The Ford had become a liability, not smart enough to belong to the fictitious friend whose home he was borrowing. It had to be kept out of Jane's sight. He made up his mind to sell it.

As he was leaving for work in the morning, Stefan caught him on the landing.

'Jim, there was a man for you. He came round twice. Saturday and again yesterday.'

'Did he leave a name?'

'No.'

'The same one that came before?'

Stefan emphasized with a shake of the head. 'No. This one was younger. Thin. The sort of eyes that don't miss anything. He didn't go near Geordie and he didn't ask to go in your room or anything.'

'I guess you told him what time I get in on week days.'

'He kept on, saying he had to see you and how important it was.'

'Well, if he comes by again don't tell him anything else. OK?'

Jim took the car to work. If the police were calling at Tubbs Road – not Boulter who'd got nowhere on his visits but a different detective who might be quicker witted – then Jim was going to keep out of the way. He left the Ford in a back street and arrived outside the shop as a man crouched in the doorway.

The wind was lifting a strip of hair brushed across a bald pate. Eric Shaw twisted to see who'd come up to him. For an instant it wasn't the face Jim knew, it was that of a frightened man. Then Shaw recovered, saying: 'I suppose it would be far too much trouble for you to offer a hand with this? I have arthritis, you know.'

'No, I didn't know, Eric. OK, let me try.' He wriggled the key in the lock. Then he squatted down to get on eye level with the problem.

'Oh, hurry up.' Shaw smoothed the strip of hair back into place. 'We're late opening as it is. They cancelled my bus. I presume one of their drivers couldn't be bothered to get out of bed.'

Jim stood up. 'The key's turned, Eric. There has to be another reason the door isn't opening.'

'Oh, let me get there.' Shaw barged him out of the way and investigated the lock himself, peering into it with his glasses on and then again with them pushed up on to his head. He rattled the door. He was red and angry. 'This is ridiculous.'

'How about the bolts?' suggested Jim. 'If the bolts are shot that would explain it.'

'Quite. But we don't use those bolts. We lock and bolt the back door and we come out this way and lock up with the keys. That's the way it's always been done.'

Jim was entertained by the spectacle of Eric Shaw steaming towards a public tantrum. 'The bolts are my best guess. What's yours? Superglue?'

Inside the shop a telephone rang. Shaw struck the window with his fist. He ranted about the frustration and the absurdity.

Jim said: 'That won't be a customer, not before nine. It's probably one of the staff ringing in sick.'

'Is that supposed to improve matters, Jim?'

'Have you tried round the back?'

'The *back*?'

'Perhaps there was a mistake and the front door was bolted

on Saturday instead of the back one. We might find we can walk right in that way.'

Shaw muttered imprecations about the unreliability of Daphne, the woman entrusted with the keys on Saturdays when he took his day off. But he set off to the rear yard, saying Jim was to stay at the front door and explain to any of the staff who deigned to put in an appearance.

A bus swept along the street and Jim saw Daphne alight. 'Oh Gawd,' she said when he told her. 'Eric will be on the rampage all week after this lot.'

'You're quite sure you . . .'

'Gawd, don't you start, Jim. Of course I bloody locked up the right way. Been doing it long enough, haven't I?' She tried the door, then: 'Well, he says one word out of place to me and I'm giving my notice. My Jack's been telling me for ages. "Why bother, Daphne?" he says. And I've had an offer from the baker round where I live. I could pick up another bit of shop work easy.'

Jim posted Daphne by the front door and went round the back. The back door was also bolted.

He said: 'We have to break in.'

'We can't,' said Shaw. 'We're wired to the police station.'

'Telephone them first.'

Shaw was hysterical. 'Oh yes, brilliant. I ring up and tell the desk sergeant I'm the manager of a shop full of valuable electrical goods and I'm about to smash my way in and please would the police ignore the alarm bells. What fool would believe that story? They'd have a squad car here before the broken glass landed on the doormat.'

Jim gritted his teeth. 'Maybe I should go to the snack bar and leave you to deal with this on your own.'

'Quite frankly, Jim, you might as well for all the help you're being.'

'OK, if that's what you want.' He walked away.

Shaw ran after him. 'All right, I'll phone the police. They might send someone to help us get in. I'll ask to borrow Potter's phone.' Potter was the men's outfitter several doors away.

The police disappointed Shaw by being too busy to send

immediate assistance. Daphne, Jim and the diffident school leaver called Ron who helped in the shop, saw him strutting towards them overflowing with self-importance.

'We'll have to take matters into our own hands,' he said, and detailed Jim and Ron to accompany him to the yard.

'No chance,' said Jim examining the office window. 'Not without borrowing a hacksaw from the DIY place. We're never going to bend those bars.'

The security grille on the door and the bars on the first- and second-floor windows were equally defensive. They looked up at the back of the building, its fabric neglected and in need of repointing. All the premises in the terrace were the same: attention was lavished on ground-floor shop fronts and the rest was left to crumble.

Jim said: 'How would it be if we went through the third-floor window?'

'Impossible,' said Shaw. 'Unless, of course, you carry crampons around with you.'

Ron gave an unguarded laugh, mistaking sarcasm for wit. He covered it with a cough. Then: 'No, it's too high, Jim. That's why there aren't any bars on that window. Eric's right, we couldn't get up there.'

'I reckon I could.'

He enjoyed the next few minutes, loved the look on their faces as he unfolded his plan. 'I'll need to move one of the vans,' he began.

The keys had been dropped through the front letterbox and were inaccessible. He broke into a van, connected wires and started the engine. Once the van was alongside the high wall that cut the yard off from its neighbours, he lifted the ladder out of the back and handed it to Ron. Then Jim took a tyre lever from the repair kit, tucked it into his belt, jumped from the bonnet of the van to the roof of it, and on to the wall. On the far side was a similar yard.

Where it abutted the next building, the wall broadened from two bricks' width to a buttressing pier. Jim stood on that and considered the angle between the wall of the build-ing and the furthest edge of the pier. He gestured to Ron to pass the ladder.

When he was a quarter of the way up the ladder, Jim became scared. He couldn't stop thinking about his fall the day the dog dislodged him. His skin grew clammy. The ladder he was on seemed almost vertical, its feet were precariously near the edge of the pier. Below he saw two upturned faces, each with the look of a man in an accident crowd. He didn't put it past Eric Shaw to be willing him to break his arrogant neck. He urged himself on.

As he passed beyond the first section of the ladder, he sensed a tremor. Jim rested, waiting for the movement to stop. But when he transferred his weight to the next rung, he felt it again. Another rung. More wobble. Sweat ran into his hairline, his hands were slippery. He'd never been nervous of heights, he'd never believed he could fall; but he had. What had happened once could happen again. He bullied himself to ignore his body's panic signals and to go on.

He reached the second-floor window, its sill potentially useful: if the ladder fell, it needn't follow that he fell too. Jim wiped his hands against his shirt, gripped the ladder and made a little more headway. But the ladder was unsteady. He ran his tongue over parched lips and called down: 'Ron? Would you hold the bottom of the ladder?'

Ron scrambled on to the van and hoisted himself on to the wall. Jim set a steady pace and trusted to Ron, to luck and to his own calculation about the angle. The second section went by. He experienced slight judders but carried on. There was nothing else to be done except aim for the third-floor window sill.

And then he was close. The ladder ran up beside the window. He rested a hand on the sill, steadied his breath and drew out the tyre lever. He smashed the upper pane, near the central catch. Then he tapped away glass, lay the lever on the sill and reached an arm into the space. He was about to discover whether it had been a good idea after all.

Unused windows get painted up, nailed, fitted with locks, or are just cussedly impossible to shift. The catch was intractable. A head stuck out of a window a few buildings along and a woman who'd been disturbed by his noise shouted at him. He ignored her, attacked the lower pane with the lever, breaking off pieces and then chipping and clearing what was left. He climbed through.

His shoes splintered glass. A kitchen sink stood in a corner and an ancient gas stove on the landing. He saw nothing connected with J. and J. until he descended to the first-floor landing and boxes of small electrical appliances: hair-dryers, toasters, shavers.

Jim shoved back the door to the big room at the front where stock was stored. The mess indicated the shop had been busy on Saturday. He ran down the remaining stairs, opened the back door to Shaw and Ron and then the front one to Daphne and the others. Three customers were waiting, fascinated by the proceedings.

'Mission accomplished,' said Jim, chirpy now the danger was over.

Shaw was withering. 'You'd better get on to the glass fitters immediately.' He flustered everybody with his attempts to restore a calm and businesslike atmosphere.

Ron was regaling Daphne and the customers with tales of Jim's daring but Shaw had had enough of it. 'That'll do, Ron. I'm sure everyone realizes our installers are capable of climbing ladders.' He added that he was going upstairs to inspect the damaged window.

'That mean old . . .' Ron began as soon as Shaw was out of sight.

Daphne said: 'I reckon you done very well, Jim. We'd all be stood out on the pavement if we'd waited for Eric bloody Shaw to think of something, wouldn't we?'

Jim asked her: 'Where's Alex?'

She lowered her voice. 'Oh Gawd.'

His mouth tightened to a mean line. 'When did it happen?'

She looked to where the customers were browsing by the television sets, the coffee-makers and the microwave ovens. Out of earshot. She said: 'Friday afternoon. Eric called me into the office to tell me officially, as I'm supposed to be deputy while he's running things. Obviously we all knew because we heard every word. Ron reckoned they must have heard it as far down the road as the Indian take-away.'

She paused to answer a question about the special offer

on an oven before saying: 'Anyway, I said to Eric that I hoped he was sure about Alex because sacking's a serious matter. And he said he was perfectly sure, thank you very much, and there was no need for me to concern myself.'

The noise of Shaw pounding down the stairs made them break off. He burst in gabbling about a burglary. When the police came he presented them with the theory that Alex had returned between Saturday evening and Monday morning and helped himself to video equipment, televisions and hi-fi gear from the stock room. Boxes were missing and others turned out to be empty. Thousands of pounds worth of goods had been stolen.

Jim was made to explain his own role in the Monday-morning drama and registered, not without satisfaction, the creeping despair of the police sergeant as he learned that everyone on the premises had been at least once to poke around in the stock room and add their penn'orth of opinion to Shaw's.

The detective asked Jim: 'How much do you know about the one who got the chop for nicking stuff? You worked with him more than the others did.'

'Not really. We went out on jobs separately most of the time.'

The detective added another line in his notebook. 'Do you reckon this Alex would have come back and done this job?'

'To be honest, I don't see how he could have. The reason I was doing gymnastics on that ladder was that the front and back doors were bolted on the inside.'

The man's jaw slackened a fraction. 'Nobody's mentioned that *both* doors were bolted.'

'Interesting,' said Jim.

'Are you sure nobody was in the building when you came through that window?'

'I saw nobody.'

'Well it's beginning to look as though Alex might have come out the way you went in: with a ladder.'

'You saw that window?'

The man grinned. 'The little bit you left intact.'

'Nobody went in or out of that window before I did. It's

painted up, the catch too. Besides, I have trouble imagining Alex tramping up and down a ladder carrying the videos and the televisions and . . .'

'Let's go outside and take a look.'

And when Jim showed him where he'd perched the ladder and how high and how steeply he'd climbed, he knew he'd never have been believed if it hadn't been for Ron and Eric Shaw who'd witnessed it.

The police officer tried once more to blame Alex. 'Of course, he'd have carried everything out of the back door to a van, wouldn't he?'

'The shop keys were with Daphne and with Eric Shaw. I guess Alex could have had duplicates made, but . . .'

'But what?'

'None of this sounds like anything the guy would do.'

'Life's full of surprises.' The detective shut his notebook.

Jim drove west, to Richmond, once he'd finished work for the day. He felt hedged about by problems. Whenever life became like this, his inclination was to cut and run. But how could he when any move would step up suspicion about where he came from or what he was doing or where he meant to go?

There was one sanctuary: the protected world of Jane Logan. If he could get there, he need never have this kind of trouble again. People, policemen, wouldn't pester him about his affairs or those of his acquaintances. They'd expect him to be aloof, uncommunicative, loyal. They wouldn't bother to waste their time, and if by chance circumstances forced them to approach him, then they'd be deferential as the hotel staff had been to 'Orlando', as the nightclub staff were when he talked his way in as one of Jane's set, or as the shops were when he'd ordered goods in the name of a rich man. Disposing of the hire car had demonstrated this: the chauffeur was interrogated but the police assured Jim there was no need to trouble him, and the hire company was anxious to apologize for the inconvenience he'd suffered. He'd laughed at their stupidity, their prejudice.

He parked the Ford near the Thames. Young men sculling. Birds riding the ripples. A broken chain of boys fishing from the bank. Beautiful, but he wished he were anywhere else. He was compelled to stay, to learn the worst. He telephoned the house in Queens Road.

Penny Reynoldes said yes, please, she'd meet him for a drink in half an hour. They chose a wine bar she liked, the one where he'd watched her father with his girlfriend until Penny had bounded up and he'd prevented her finding out the truth. Penny, he now suspected, could have handled the truth. She sounded delighted to hear from him although her voice was soft and conspiratorial and he was certain she wasn't going to tell her mother she was meeting him.

He walked down to the water's edge. A trio of nannies sat on a bench, children playing on the grass beside them. Five tiny boys squabbling and ineffective, one little girl self-sufficient. They recalled the Weedons, all those boys and Rosanna. He'd spent his childhood over on the Weedon place, fighting and playing and often both at once. And Rosanna, she'd been like this anonymous English child, safe within herself, unruffled by the mayhem of the boys. Boys were like flags on a gusty day: now being this, now feeling that, the victims of inconsistency. Girls arrived with an innate knowledge of how to rub along, organize themselves. They were a success from the start, and they kept it up until the age when, oh mystery, they capitulated and invited a man to play the lead in their lives.

If a guy was smart, Jim thought, he could tell when that was coming. Girls would get a doggy way about them, scenting around, reading a boy's horoscope in the magazines before their own, happening to be where he happened to go. Rosanna had got that way, and as she was right next door it was awkward. When he'd gone to see Al that time and hunted outside for him, Rosanna had trailed him into the barn. He'd been skipping out of her way for months because he'd seen guys get tangled up when friendship was refashioned by a girl into something special. He wanted out, he didn't want something special and especially not with Rosanna.

The nannies created a truce in a small war, gathered up the children and led them home. A toy lay broken and discarded, its smooth white curve of plastic visible through the grass. He blamed them for not caring, as he had cared.

He could see her face in his mind. The woman made eggs, Easter eggs of spun sugar that had the glitter and sheen of snowflakes. She looped ribbon around them, pinned fluffy chicks on the bows and sold them. He'd wanted one, above all else he'd wanted one.

She was dark, patient. She regarded him and he regarded her sugar eggs. The second year he prayed more fervently, promising Jesus not to let his mind drift during services, striking lopsided bargains so that he might be given one of the spun-sugar Easter eggs. His mother bought one secretly, lay it by his plate on Easter morning. He weighed it in his hand, its ovoid solidity comforting. When the ribbon slipped undone and the chick flopped on to the tablecloth, he rolled his egg delicately around his plate, clockwise then anti-clockwise.

His father derided. 'A farm boy and he's doting on a stupid thing like that!'

Jim didn't look up. He rolled the egg beneath his palm, this way and that. Its surface was scratchy-smooth, a bit of both. He sensed its secrets, shifting within.

His mother said: 'Mind you don't dirty that before you eat it.'

And he didn't like to tell her he was never going to eat it, that it was his beautiful prayed-for possession and he would treasure it for ever.

Weeks later his cousins came and that's how the marvellous egg was broken, in a scuffle. His own thumb it was that jabbed through the shell. He yelled out. He flung the damaged thing against the wall. It left a powdery mark as it exploded. What hurt so was the shock of emptiness, of his thumb plunging through the perfect surface to discover *nothing*.

The cousins left him to cry, ran out into the blustery day. They were older, his tears were a joke. They forgot, immediately. He couldn't ever forget that hollowness. He never saw sugar eggs again, the woman disappeared taking her spells with her.

Jim strolled to the wine bar, plagued by the idea that whatever Penny reported would make a bad day worse. He needed a drink.

The bar was popular. Commuters on their way home from London dropped in, giving themselves away by a briefcase propped against the leg of a chair. He ordered a Scotch, watched the barman at the optic. To his horror, the mirror behind it revealed an auburn-haired woman standing a yard away, on his left. He dropped his eyes to the bar top, afraid of meeting hers. The drink was set in front of him and in one smooth movement he pushed the money across, took up the glass and turned away to his right.

He wished he knew where she'd found a seat but there were no clues on the faces of the other customers. He sipped, staying near the bar, doubtful where to go. In the corner of his eye he caught a streak of grey and green linen as the woman moved. She answered his query by making for a table where two other women waited for her. That settled it, he would be safer outside. For the second time in that place, he'd save Penny from running into her father's mistress.

Penny was approaching as he stepped outside. 'Too full in there?'

He said yes and they found a spot in the shade. He got to and from the bar for her drink without mishap. On his return she asked about the plaster on his hand.

'A dog bite?' she gasped. 'Ugh. That's horrible. Did you have to have injections and things?'

'And stitches, to be precise.'

'Oh, Jim. What sort of dog was it?'

'Everybody asks about the breed of dog. If I'd been run down by a car would you all have wanted to know the make?'

'Certainly. And the model.'

'Yes, and in your case the year of registration so that you could work out what it was worth.'

She pouted, not liking his joke. 'I think I'm being repri-manded for being mercenary.'

'The truth is I don't have a neat reply to this serious ques-tion about the dog. It was a mongrel, something with large vicious genes crossed with something with bad-tempered ones.'

She shuddered, made him say where the attack had happened. He told her it was in a Hampstead street when he was visiting a friend. She shuddered some more.

Penny was on her second drink before she mentioned the investigation into the death of her father. 'The inspector on the case is being very sweet. One of Clive's father's friends knows him, so perhaps that makes a difference. Apparently they don't always give much away.'

'They don't always have much,' he suggested.

'Someone has come forward to say he thinks he saw Daddy with a man on the evening before he was found.'

He struggled for that natural level of curiosity. 'By the river?'

'No, on Richmond Hill. A car like Daddy's was facing up the hill on the wrong side and the driver was talking to a young man who got in.'

Jim frowned. 'But is there anything to confirm that it was your father's car?'

Penny said not, or at any rate that's what she understood.

'You don't sound too sure,' he said.

'I'm not sure that the police don't have other information. In fact, they gave a pretty strong hint of it but they wouldn't say what. Mummy says they'd hold things back because when they question a suspect it's better if they have a clue or two up their sleeve.'

He listened to her recapping conversations with the police and throwing in the opinions of family and friends. Soon she switched to talking about her mother, who was weakening about letting her go to the crammer.

Jim encouraged her with murmurs of interest, but in his mind's eye he was walking up Richmond Hill, being accosted by Matthew Reynoldes and forced to get into the car. He was remembering the drivers who'd been inconvenienced by Reynoldes's parking and obliged to notice the encounter. He was wondering which one had given him away.

Seven

Jane Logan slipped her arm through his. They were standing in the garden. They had the house to themselves for the weekend, her parents were on holiday. If he ignored the chimney pots of the housekeeper's cottage and the gardener's lodge, he could persuade himself they were the only people for miles.

Jane said: 'Come on, I want to show you something.' She led him by the hand.

Beyond the copse the view opened out. Yellow summer fields, a building in the middle distance, some hazy spires on the skyline. Jane took a path alongside a brambled hedge until the land sloped abruptly. She watched his surprise, said: 'Isn't it wonderful?'

'Yes, but what . . .'

She ran down the bank but he stayed on the edge. What had seemed uninterrupted acres were sliced by a massive ditch. Trees grew there, shrubs thrived in its shelter. Jane shouted up: 'Daddy calls it Dr Beeching's gift to us.'

'Dr Who?'

'No, not Dr Who, that's the other one.' She was disappearing into the greenery. He had to follow.

She said: 'Beeching's the one who axed the rural railway lines. Before he came along one could get up to London from here.'

'Who owns it now?'

'Well, not us. An odd little man from Birmingham bought it, miles and miles of it, but heaven knows why. Mummy decided after a few years that as he wasn't doing anything with it, except letting it turn into a wilderness, she'd send Dixon down here to plant it up a bit.'

She added that no one used it except the Logans. Her sister, Maddy, liked to walk the retrievers there.

They paused to watch finches fluttering around seed heads. Then Jim said: 'But why put trains down here? The land's fairly flat.'

'The Victorian Logans wouldn't have it skirt our land any other way. They said the railway could come if it chose but they were damned if they were going to have their view ruined.'

He opened his mouth to exclaim at the huge cost and trouble that must have imposed, at the high-handedness of such a demand, but he curbed himself in time. He said: 'I like railways. I used to watch the trains when I was a kid.'

'Did you have those funny trains with the high-pitched sirens? Do you know, I could never believe they were real, until I saw them for myself. They seemed more to do with old films – Westerns or Judy Garland – than with real transport.'

And he was a kid again, by a cornfield, supposed to be lending a hand with one of those repetitive tasks that fill country days. But instead he was gaping at a metal shape cleaving the fields, shaking his bones with its noise. Ever since there'd been something about trains, although nothing to equal that child's-eye view of the railroad running through Iowa.

He'd decided when he was six that one day he'd ride on the iron charger. One day he'd go out into the fields and when it came it would stop for him, a sun-browned hand would reach down to hoist him on board, and together they'd run away. That, after a fashion, was what had happened.

They'd run from white clapboard churches, red barns with kinked Dutch roofs, the silver of bullet-shaped silos catching the sun, and blacktop roads stark among dirt tracks. They'd shaken off neat towns where one-time farm suppliers sold cornhusk dollies and hand-painted saw blades to tourists. And they'd fled so fast that when the pitchfork couples straightened their backs to mark their passing, they were too distant for him to read pity in their eyes.

Jane Logan found a Red Admiral, its colours rich in the sun but its wings frayed. 'Poor thing, it won't last the day.' Delicately she lifted it from the ground to a bush, a safer place.

They went on up the disused railway line. Even when the sun was blocked by a purple cloud, she led him on saying there was another way to the house. Rain rattled on the leaves soon after. They moved into the shelter of a tree and he enfolded her in his arms as if for protection. They kissed.

In a while he said: 'I guess we're going to have to get out there and face the weather.'

'Oh no, it'll soon blow over.'

They remained beneath the tree, kissing. Her slender fingers stroked his face. 'You're so beautiful,' she said.

But he was thinking of the butterfly, beautiful but damaged. Perhaps beauty was never enough. He pictured the darting rain crushing it.

Rain penetrated the leaves and dark stains appeared on his shirtsleeves, on her blouse. Huddled, they ran for the house. The incline to the garden was slippery. As he held out his hand and pulled her the last slithering yard, thunder growled.

'This way.' She dashed past him, her skirt limp and heavy around her legs. The path zig-zagged through a shrubbery, a few seconds' worth of running before she flung herself at the door of a summerhouse. Jane spun round, squealing as he leaped across the veranda after her.

'My God,' she cried. 'I've never been so wet.'

He rubbed a handkerchief over his face, she was doing things to her hair. He was by the door. On a clear day there would be an extensive view to the hint of a market town. Rain foreshortened it to a blur of green, flashing white as water tipped from the shale roof and pooled in front of the veranda.

He turned to comment on it. She was standing in the middle of the summerhouse, naked to the waist, using her blouse to squeeze moisture from her hair. She tossed the blouse aside and went to him and put her arms around his neck.

'Storms are rather exciting, don't you think, James?'

He pushed her away, slightly, to allow him to take the weight of her breasts in his hands. Her skin was cold. He said: 'Is it all right here?'

She giggled that it was all right anywhere. And silenced his misgivings with another of her lingering kisses.

They made love without interruption from gardeners or housekeepers, without being joined by anyone else in need of shelter from the storm. His fleeting doubts had been unnecessary, but it was not his favourite time with her. He came too quickly, a pleasure snatched instead of savoured.

Afterwards, as she sat cross-legged on the floor buttoning her blouse, she teased him. 'You really do prefer it in a big warm bed, don't you, James?'

A shirt button had come off. He was trying to find where it had rolled.

She said: 'I like it out of doors. That's what the countryside is for, didn't you know?'

He'd located the button. It was against the wall, beneath a table. He said over his shoulder: 'Outside's fine. Maybe I have a hang-up about English summerhouses.' And barns, he thought, especially barns.

Thunder was closer and the pressure of rain increased. Jane said: 'Oh Lord, it's getting worse.'

His turn to tease. 'I thought you found it exciting.'

'For ten minutes or so, but I've got Hilly coming round and there'll be no one at the house.'

'Who,' he asked, his spirits sinking, 'is Hilly?' Obviously it was another of the fragments of her social life that he'd have to jigsaw into place.

She was plaiting her hair, smoothing and twisting it. 'A neighbour.'

'I thought you didn't have any.' He meant people who lived next door, not like-minded people anywhere within five miles.

She cast a sideways glance. 'Sorry, James. I know I said we'd have the place to ourselves but I couldn't say no to Hilly. He's a pet, he's being kind to his cousin's friend who's in the country for a week or two and . . .'

146

He wasn't clear whether this time she meant in England or whether she meant any part of Britain that wasn't London. Sometimes she used country one way, sometimes the other. Thinking about it, he missed a chunk of her explanation and a response was required. 'So Hilly's coming on his own?'

'*No*, he's bringing his cousin's friend. Just for a drink, around six.'

'Jane, it's gone five thirty.'

'We'll have to dash out into the wet again. Do you mind awfully?'

Hilly was younger and more interesting than Jane had made him sound. He'd travelled and he'd spent a year at an American university. Ordinarily, talking to him would have been easy. In fact it was like ducking repeated invitations to traipse across a minefield. Jim left Hilly to Jane and concentrated on the cousin's friend. This was an angular Australian woman, nearing forty. As she was happy to recite details of her unadventurous journeying, she threatened nothing but boredom. Trained to the minute, the pair were on their feet and making their exit soon after the longcase clock in the entrance hall chimed seven.

When they'd driven off Jane said: 'I *must* make a phone call.'

Jim poured himself another drink and sank into a chintz armchair. The room was amazing, the whole house was.

Sixteenth century red brick softened by dilapidation. Uncertain gateposts balancing granite balls. Linen-fold panelling, massive fireplaces, and centuries of wax polish on an oak staircase.

From the telephone in the hall he heard Jane. 'Petra? Jane here. Look, the thing is, Hilly's been over and . . . Oh, you already know? I was going to warn you . . . Weeks, apparently. He fears she's taken root . . . Yes, well rescue him if you can, my sweet. Even Hilly doesn't deserve this . . . Mmm . . . Oh could we? Wonderful . . . See you soon. Bye.'

She looked mischievous when she appeared in the doorway. 'That was my friend Petra, the one who breeds racehorses. We're joining her tonight at the Swan.' She went to warn the housekeeper.

Their time together was invariably shared by her friends, either in the flesh or on the telephone. Even when they were in her car she made calls. It undermined his confidence in her affection for him.

There were eight of these friends at the Swan. At first he thought the occasion was a celebration, a birthday or anniversary perhaps, but it wasn't. Petra and her friends went there frequently. Jim knew two of the men from the London nightclub, and also keen-eyed Caroline and her husband, Simon, who revived the offer to take Jim sailing.

Fortunately, the conversation was dominated by Petra and her horses, but Jim found the evening a strain, feeling Caroline's interest in him and knowing they'd pick over everything he'd said or not said, the impression he'd given or failed to give. He pulled himself together. People always discussed new acquaintances. Besides, it was Jane who mattered. But he regretted diving so deep in this social pool. The challenge had been fun in London but on Jane's home ground he couldn't fool himself that he had a hand on the controls.

When they had given up dawdling over brandies and were in the car park, he breathed relief. He unlocked Jane's car and looked around for her. She was with Petra and Petra's man, and they were holding long-distance conversations with the others across the roofs of cars. Jim spared a thought for people trying to sleep in the hotel, the emphatic clarity of Simon's consonants ensured that at least one contribution to the conversation was loud and clear. Then he caught the drift.

He got into the car in lip-biting anger. She might have *asked*. Oh, what the hell, he'd have said yes. What other answer was open to him? But she was always . . .

Jane bounced into the passenger seat. 'I've invited them to . . .'

'Yes, I heard.' Edgy, no disguising it.

'What's up with you? I thought it was a good idea.'

He patted her hand. 'Yes, yes, Jane, of course it is. I guess I'm tired, nothing more.'

'Are you fit to drive?'

He said yes. Because of the minefields he hadn't drunk much, he had to be careful in every way.

Jane drew his face down to hers and kissed him. 'I'll see they don't stay long.'

But they did. They drank and they talked and one of the men Jim had met at the nightclub tipped white powder on to the mantelpiece. He used his gold credit card to spread it and cut it into lines.

Jim stuck with brandy. He wished to escape from them, if only to the other end of the room, but the trick was always to fit in. He lounged on the chintz, with the air of one as happy as Jane herself.

Petra came and knelt on the old Chinese rug in front of him. Despite make-up and sophisticated dressing, she'd never throw off the outdoor look. From beneath a frizz of baby-fine honey-coloured hair she said: 'I've been talking to Jane about you, James.' The hours of drinking had had an effect on her.

He was quizzical.

She smothered a chuckle. 'But she says I can't have you.'

'Have you come for a second opinion?'

She thought that witty. Then: 'No, but seriously, she was telling me about the Rushwoods.'

'Ah.' Dangerous territory indeed. Yet he must make her repeat Jane's words. 'How much did she tell you?'

Curiously, what Jane had said was more elaborate than what he'd told Jane. Unless Petra herself was exaggerating it? He doubted that, she was too drunk. *In vino veritas*, and so forth.

'Well,' he said, dismissing the Norfolk Rushwoods by a gesture with his brandy glass. 'I guess they haven't been around here for a good long while.'

'But Jim, my mother was connected to them. You see? We're practically relations.'

'Is that so?' And then he shunted trouble down a siding with a joke. 'In that case you definitely can't have me.'

Petra collapsed into tearful laughter. She had to tell someone, she really did. She stumbled to her feet and sought a listener. Jim allowed a respectable pause and then went out to the kitchen hoping Jane had made coffee. It had been mooted a long while earlier, before the cocaine appeared.

But there was no coffee in the pot. He poked around for a can of ground coffee, or beans, anything. And when he'd wasted time this way he went in search of Jane. She seemed not to be downstairs. As he went up he heard voices.

One of the women was saying: 'I must say you've gone for looks this time. He's absolutely gorgeous.'

And Jane: 'Oh, he's more interesting than that.'

A giggle. 'I did wonder. When they're as beautiful as that I always do wonder.'

Jane, defensive: 'James is fine.'

'All right, forget I ever wondered. But how's Felix taking it, you running around with a beautiful stud?'

They were both giggling. Then Jane: 'I'd say it was none of his business.'

'Hmm. *You* might, but I can't see old Felix agreeing with that. I mean, after all . . .'

'It's still not his business.'

'Has he got money?'

'James? Why? Do you think he hasn't?'

'Oh, take no notice, that's another example of my automatic wondering. I meet a man, I wonder if he's rich, what he's like in bed . . .'

'You're being jolly vulgar tonight.'

'Oops, sorry. Didn't know you'd become sensitive about discussing your lovers' performances.'

'I'm not, I mean your awful harping on about money. Not the done thing, remember.'

They laughed, apparently at a common memory because the other woman said: 'God yes, remember Miss Elis? "Nice girls never discuss a man's money." And when I told my mother she said: "Quite true, dear, but they count it all the same." '

When the laughter ended she added: 'Caroline thinks you ought to be careful.'

Jane came in quickly. 'He's related to the Rushwoods, that always means money. You and Caroline can stop worrying about me and let me enjoy James while he lasts.'

'You make him sound like a snowman. A beautiful sexy snowman.'

'That's how it will be. He doesn't belong here and he'll go away. I'm not even imagining keeping him. James is very much a short-term offer. Now, come on. Which of these would you like to take?'

The subject was lost in a discussion of borrowing and lending. Jim ransacked the kitchen until he came upon a bag of coffee.

Simon rang him in the morning and asked whether he'd like to sail that day. 'She's on a half-tide mooring so we'll have to leave by noon or we'll miss the tide. Think you can make it? By the way, James, Adrian's coming too. He often crews for me.'

Jane was subdued as they drove over for brunch at Simon's and Caroline's house on the coast. She screwed her eyes against a sunshine that varnished ivy on tree trunks and brought a sheen to every surface, but she denied a headache.

As the knapped-flint walls of the house appeared above a shielding hawthorn hedge, she slowed the car to a crawl. 'You don't have to do it. We can leave early, claim we have to get back to London.'

'Not sail? I'm looking forward to it.' And the sooner the better, the less time under Caroline's scrutiny the happier he'd be. Simon had always been affable and Adrian was a quiet type who'd never shown any interest in him.

He spent a tricky hour dodging Caroline, hoping Roland wouldn't renew his quiz about Camilla, and tacitly begging Petra not to dwell on the Rushwoods.

Adrian was late. Jim and Simon went down to the creek and waited for him there, with Simon on board the sloop checking the oil and hanking on the headsail while Jim returned to shore in the tender. Simon was clock-watching and tetchy. The tide would turn in three hours and they must get away soon if they were to cover any distance. There was ice in the breath of the wind.

Simon stood on the deck, hands on hips, an outline of annoyance. Jim shrugged, he'd suggested they went alone but Simon had been unenthusiastic. They were too far apart for discussion and Jim was thinking of paddling the tender nearer. Just then a sports car rumbled down the gravel track. Adrian appeared, greenish. Jim ferried him across.

Jim expected to lend a hand, wanted to, but Simon preferred him out of the way. He put it down to the big man's petulance at the delay, and went below.

Simon had spread a chart on the table. Jim picked out the mooring, the web of creeks to be negotiated before *Flying Free* achieved the open sea. Above he heard Simon's voice, the sound of lines straining, footfalls on the deck. Through a porthole he saw saltings, a gingery carr-stone cottage, yachts snatching at their moorings and the smooth plane of a sandy ridge. It was all going by, fast.

And in a while he felt *Flying Free* surge and lift, a breeze thwacking into her as she left the protection of the land and headed out into the North Sea. The porthole showed him a greyish sky laced with ribbons of sunlight, a pewter sea.

Simon called down the hatch. 'You're safe to come up now, James, without getting cursed or trodden on.'

Jim went up. Adrian was at the tiller, the wind and exertion had teased colour into his cheeks but he continued to look like a bad case of hangover. He said nothing while Simon pointed out landmarks and then showed off the boat to Jim. It wasn't the most exciting boat Jim had ever been on, but he didn't let Simon see that.

Simon said to Adrian: 'You OK for a while?'

'Fine.' Adrian tried to look alert.

'Let's go below, James.'

There seemed very little space once Simon was in the cabin. He filled a kettle and lit a stove that hung on gimbals, defying the motion of the boat. While water boiled he squeezed in behind the chart table. 'You saw this lot we had to weave through? Real *Riddle of the Sands* stuff, eh?'

'I wouldn't care to navigate it in the dark.'

'Nor me, the bar's forever shifting.' He considered the mapped coastline for a minute before asking: 'What sort of sailing have you done, James?'

He played safe. 'Not much. Dinghies mainly. The stuff kids do on holidays.'

'In Connecticut, wasn't it?'

'We used to head up into Maine. Or maybe sail the Lakes.'

The kettle began to hiss. Simon said: 'Adrian's request: a nice cup of tea. He's not at his best.'

Jim reverted to the chart. 'What's our course?'

When the tea was made he carried a mug up to Adrian and sat beside him in the stern. Simon had been probing. Jim had turned the conversation, as he invariably did in these circumstances, but Simon had bounded back. The questions had been no tougher than those regarding Jim's experience as a sailor, yet cumulatively they were troubling because they reached into every area of Jim's life. Too late he regretted accepting the invitation. Ashore he could break off, leave if it came to that. Instead he'd walked into a trap.

Adrian didn't help. He moaned about his headache and sent Jim to the cabin to ask for painkillers. Simon searched for them and introduced Jane into the conversation.

She'd been there all along, naturally, unnamed but at the front of their minds. Jim swung that subject away from himself too. 'How long have you known her, Simon?'

Facing him with the painkillers in his hand, Simon said: 'All her life. She's my cousin.'

Jim ignored the challenge in his eyes, reminiscent now of Caroline's. He delivered the tablets to Adrian and remained, staring towards land, thinking: 'So that's it then. The family's checking up. Fairly crudely at that. Well, at any rate I know now.'

He took the tiller to allow Adrian to drink his tea and lament the good time he'd enjoyed the night before at a party. Simon came up and said they were to change course. Rather than accept Jim's help, Simon again excluded him. Far more than any of Jane's set had ever done, Simon treated him as an outsider. Jim went below while they tacked.

He stretched out on a bunk and pretended that it was his boat, that up on deck his crew were sailing him away to . . . Where? Freedom, anyhow. He'd never owned a boat, not truly although people had been encouraged to think he did.

That was in Florida, an adventure that became altogether too adventurous when the customs boats gave chase. And since then . . .

Flying Free heeled. Jim opened an eye. She was at an alarming angle, the porthole beside him showed only the sky. But the shafts of sunshine had gone, sky and sea were now the same threatening grey. He rested on one elbow and watched, questioning how long Simon would let the wind press her. Why didn't he put a reef in?

Again she heeled. Jim's weight shifted and he braced an arm against the dining table to prevent himself falling into the gap between that and the bunk. Twisting, he got his feet to the floor.

Waves were slamming between the keels, crashing over the foredeck. As they tacked, he heard Simon's cry above the sound of the jib savaged by the wind. The amount of noise was terrifying.

In the cabin the packet of painkillers fell from the table, slid along the teak floor. Jim picked it up, grabbing at a shelf to steady himself, missing and being hurled across to a bunk. He drew himself upright, holding on to anything that came to hand, and he strapped on a safety harness. Then he scrambled up through the hatch.

Rain slashed his face. Adrian and Simon were struggling for control but the wind was cheating them, attacking this way and that. Simon was at the starboard winch, hardening in on the headsail. Jim attempted to help but Simon shoved him aside. Beyond him Jim saw Adrian, doubled, no longer steering, gripping the tiller but intent on nothing but his pain.

As the boat came off the top of a wave, he let her slew across the wind. A gust caught her, threw her on to her beam ends, and Simon slipped, bounced against the lifelines. Crabwise, moving fast, Jim went for Adrian. The fool had to ease the helm, he *must*.

And as Jim reached him, Adrian released his grip and Jim took the tiller and brought the boat back on to the wind. Jim held her there. Beside him Adrian slumped, nursing his head. Then he sank to his knees and crawled across the

154

heaving cockpit to drop through the hatch into the security of the cabin. Jim watched Simon on the winch and tried very hard to believe that the sails were responding and the craft was safe.

Simon shouted: 'I'm turning for home. No use going on in this.'

'Better put a reef in, we have too much sail.'

Simon took the helm. 'No, we'll have the wind behind us. Anyway, we weren't forecast anything worse than a force five.'

And they were running before the wind when there was the crash of the boom swinging across, then the explosive, worst sound of the mast snapping, and the smash of the sail hitting the water. Jim clambered across a tangle of halyards and shrouds. The mast was grinding alongside the boat, cutting into her topsides. They had to cut it clear or drag it on board before it holed the hull.

They dragged.

She was pitching, the mast and waterlogged sail were heavy and awkward. They managed to get lines around them and winch, but it took time. They didn't *have* much time. She was drifting towards the shore, where the breaking waves would pound her to pieces. There was a barn, a church tower above a beach. They were getting nearer.

Jim was still bent over the mast, finishing lashing, when behind him he heard the engine rasp, settle to a steady rhythm. Then it cut out.

He looked round. There was too much commotion of wind and water for him to hear Simon's curses. Jim looked towards the shore. He could see a fence near the barn, make out a window in the tower. The little share of time was running out, the wind was pushing them towards disaster. He finished the knot, with care worked his way down into the cockpit.

Jim said: 'It has to be a line in the propeller.'

'For Christ's sake! It's obviously a line.'

They tried the boat-hook first, hoping to snatch the end of the line and draw it off the propeller shaft. Then they turned the engine over backwards by hand with the decompression lifters open. But that didn't work either.

Jim said: 'Get a knife.'

'We could try turning it once more.'

'Depends how keen you are to be beaten to pulp on the shore. Come on, there isn't time to argue.'

Simon let him do it. He found the knife, a snorkel and mask, a safety line, and he let Jim lower himself over the side and free the fouled propeller. It wasn't a quick job, it was difficult, dangerous and exhausting. When Jim heaved himself back on board, cows were visible in a field in front of the barn, and a white owl flew through the gaping window in the barn. The engine fired within minutes of shipwreck.

They turned for home. *Flying Free* could make six and a half knots in fair weather, but in this barely four. Jim suggested they put in at the nearest anchorage.

Early evening but a lowering sky and once or twice the sting of rain in the wind. Lights were coming on in houses, but none of the buoys and leading marks that guided sailors into the network of creeks could be lit. Time was running out again. The light was going, the water too.

But Simon said: 'I feel safer on this coast using the places I know best.'

'Wasn't there a proper harbour at . . . ?' He couldn't think of the name but he'd seen it on the chart: a real harbour with a lit entrance and sheltered water.

Simon knew where he meant but argued against it. 'Look, it's not as though there's anything wrong with the engine. I say we push on.' He added: 'Anyway, it's looking clearer ahead.'

The shoreline was different on the return journey. Roads and cottages that had seemed built at the waterside lay beyond acres of silt. The broad stretches of water had run away and all that remained were narrow streams oozing through sandy valleys.

Simon took the tiller for the last leg. Tense, they watched the depth-sounder as she reached the bar, waves breaking around her. Briefly her keels brushed the bottom, but then she was lifted free and they knew the relief of entering calm water.

Flying Free nosed into a creek. Around a bend it widened but a row of withies marked the deep channel. Simon watched the depth-sounder. He'd been justified in fretting about water levels. The boat had twin keels, a draught of three feet, but there was every likelihood of her grounding.

He followed a fork into a more slender creek. Within feet of her passage, yachts that had been afloat when *Flying Free* set sail were settling to the mud at their makeshift moorings. Time and again the depth-sounder confirmed what was plain to the eye: she was going to be very lucky to make it without grounding.

But finally Simon glided her close to her mooring and cut the engine. Jim was making fast the mooring chain when Adrian surfaced again to inquire: 'Are we back? Oh, thank God for that.'

He came on deck and got under their feet as they tidied and took stock, pulled the tender close and lowered into it things to go ashore. Simon asked Adrian to make the first trip with it, and when he was paddling away, he called Jim below.

'Look,' he said, 'I'd rather no one said too much to Caroline and the others about what happened out there.'

'You can't keep a broken mast secret!'

'No, but they needn't know we made quite such a pig's ear of it. Need they?'

Jim kept him waiting a thoughtful moment before agreeing. 'I doubt if we'll need to mention that.'

Simon dropped the chart back in its drawer. He understood. 'Thanks, James,' he said solemnly. 'Thanks for everything.'

Jim was taking money from Jane's friend Jo-Jo. This was easy because he didn't like the man and because Jo-Jo's addiction to gambling wasn't matched by skill. Jim would go to the tables early and play for an hour before joining Jane and her friends in the nightclub next door. After a few weeks, Jo-Jo asked Jim whether he knew the Bellringer Club, and took him there. At the Bellringer there was the chance of a game with better players and higher stakes.

Win or lose, Jo-Jo was impervious to fortune, having so much of the other kind of fortune that it hardly mattered whether he were a few thousand pounds up or down on the night. Jim lost, broke even, won. Then he hit a lucky streak.

He favoured one particular table, the croupier a vacuous young woman, all chiffon and fishnet. He'd flash her a smile from his deep blue eyes and her lips would part over a set of perfect crowns. Then attention would be on her hands, stumpy but well manicured, the red nails glittering as she conjured fate. Jo-Jo never received her hint of a smile, nor did the others. The smile fuelled Jim's confidence.

Around his fifth or sixth visit to the Bellringer she was replaced by a lacquered lady in plunging black. His luck changed. For all his experience, he felt he had to prove himself to this new croupier. But her shut-in face as she pushed the chips around told him the fun was over.

In Las Vegas he'd been on her side of the table. He was aware how a croupier could upset the equilibrium, use demeanour to challenge a player, encourage one man to stay in and another to quit. How, when it came right down to it, you could cheat.

The lacquered lady was going through her paces all right. An archetypal Birmingham businessman gave up, a Greek from north London followed him. Her subtle encouragement was extended to Jo-Jo, the man known to have a limitless piggy-bank to feed his habit. But Jo-Jo was like the dummies in Las Vegas who either couldn't interpret the signs or else refused to believe them. Jim didn't understand why, but he wanted Jo-Jo to stop before he sustained a major loss. This was absurd, what else had he been doing himself but milking Jo-Jo?

Jim played on, confirming his opinion that the croupiers had been switched so that this bitch could assume the role of Lady Luck. As his winnings drained away, his resentment deepened. The loss didn't trouble him, but being taken for a fool did. He kept watch on Jo-Jo, the man's game unchanged.

And then she did it, as he knew they often did. She made

a move ahead of time. Her hand went where it ought not to have gone unless she had magical foresight. Or she was cheating.

'Oh excuse me, miss.' He was going for the very soft but determined approach.

Her stony face lifted.

He said: 'Would you mind explaining why you did that?'

'Did what?'

'Well, we were in play and you . . .' He demonstrated her gesture.

'Sir, if you have a complaint . . .' She left it hanging, expected him to decline, in a nice English way, to make a fuss.

'Sure,' he said. 'I guess we ought to send for the manager.'

Jo-Jo was incapable of grasping what was happening or why. Jim nodded to him, a non-committal acknowledgement that his presence wasn't forgotten. He hoped that when the matter was opened up to scrutiny, Jo-Jo wouldn't side with the house rather than observe an un-English fuss. The strangers at the table gave Jim more assurance than Jo-Jo did.

The manager appeared. A slick Frenchman who made a living from the business of winning and losing, it took him thirty seconds to capitulate. He wasn't asked for an admission that the Bellringer had marked Jo-Jo down and were going for the kill, he was asked to bring back chiffon and fishnet.

She strutted over in her impossibly high heels, her face flushed. When her eyes met Jim's, there was humour and her lips parted so that her crowns could gently bite her rose pink lower lip. He played a waiting game, won a little. Then he placed a far higher bet, and Jo-Jo followed his lead. Breath was held, red nails twinkled and chips flowed towards him. Jim played once more, for a smaller sum, won again and then pushed back his chair. With willpower, he coerced Jo-Jo to do the same. The manager was polite as they left.

Jim had ordered a taxi, a licensed black cab because he didn't trust drivers of the other kind. Jo-Jo had put him wise to that the first time they'd been to the Bellringer, saying a cabby called to a club would expect to be carrying passengers loaded with cash, and some of the people who posed as cab drivers were none too scrupulous.

Privately, Jim disbelieved this: most drivers called to clubs would realize they'd be carrying losers. But he'd taken Jo-Jo's advice and each time they left they used a black cab.

The taxi was waiting. The driver looked fortyish, average build, nothing to arouse suspicion in his appearance or behaviour. Jim spoke to him, got in. They drove off, to drop Jo-Jo first.

Part of their route was a rat run through ugliness. Empty shops plastered with posters advertising rock groups, sex shops leering neon, betting shops sleazy behind painted windows, grocers' shops cowering behind metal shutters, and slumped against lamp posts were plastic bags of fetid rubbish that cats . . .

A van lurched from the kerbside. Swearing, the cab driver threw himself on the brake pedal. Jim and Jo-Jo bounced from the rear seats, Jim raising an arm to protect his head as he crashed forward against the driver's compartment. He saw Jo-Jo flail for a grab handle, next saw him cradling his head. Through the rear window came the lights of another vehicle.

The taxi doors were torn open, Jim was dragged from the floor of the cab on to the road. Two pairs of feet by his face, others the far side of the cab where Jo-Jo was groaning.

Hands dragged Jim up until he was half-sitting, propped against the vehicle. A voice said: 'Give.'

Jim groped for his inside pocket. He'd heard that voice before. He raised his eyes above the level of the denims, above the black sweatshirt, and he looked into the face of the man who'd ambushed him in Soho one Saturday at the beginning of summer. He'd likened him to a dog trained to do another man's fighting. Muscular, tall and broad. And this time he carried a gun.

'Christ!' the man said. 'Look what we've got here.'

The other one said: 'What's that then?'

'O'Malley's kid, that's who. The one who reckons to do a solo on our patch and walk.'

Jim withdrew his hand. 'That's all I'm carrying.' He slid

into his slick New York accent, he'd used it on the big man before and the detail might matter.

The wodge of notes in his hand was slim, disappointing. The big man snatched it, saying: 'That's a start. Now where's the rest? You want us to shake you upside down until it all falls out?'

'There's nothing going to fall out. I owed money to guys at the club and I paid it. Whoever tells you otherwise is wrong.'

'Oh yeah? Well I say you left the Bellringer loaded. *Real* money.'

Jim started to get up. A hand thrust him down. He said: 'They were real debts. I paid them off.'

'I don't think we believe this.'

The hand left Jim's shoulder. They let him stand. Jim said: 'Listen, I went into the john and two of those guys came through and said it was time I settled. They meant it. If you want to roll a guy on his way home from the tables tonight, you picked the wrong one.'

He didn't resist as they felt through his pockets. When they'd found no more cash, and they'd thrown everything else on the ground, they faltered.

A man bawled from the car that had closed in behind the taxi. 'Get a move on, or I'm getting out of here.'

'Yeah, all right,' the big man shouted. His companion dashed to the car. The van had already gone.

The gun was jabbed up under Jim's chin. He scented beer. 'You'll be hearing,' said the man. 'I don't know why I don't take you in now. That hire-car job, that was a bad bit of business. O'Malley reckons it was down to you.'

The driver again: 'Come *on*.' He was revving, slipping the clutch, inching back.

The man jerked the gun. The barrel bruised flesh, pain seared a nerve. 'Be seeing you, Jim. Expect a visit.'

He ran, fast despite his weight, and dived into the back seat of the car. It raced, back door flapping and the man's legs protruding.

Jim touched his throat. It was sore when he swallowed. Then he became aware of the taxi driver. On reflex Jim leaned into the cab and cut the connection. 'Please don't do that. It's over, they've gone.'

The man glanced from Jim's decisiveness to Jo-Jo's shocked incoherence. 'Well, I . . . Yeah, if I radio for the police they aren't going to catch anybody, are they?'

'And you'd be kept hanging around when you could be on the road working.'

'That's about right.' The driver got out of the cab and looked up the empty street. 'I tell you, that's the last time I do a pick-up at one of those places. Beyond the call of duty, that was.'

Jim gathered up his credit cards, pens and bits and pieces from the roadway. Then he joined Jo-Jo in the cab and brushed street dirt off his trousers. 'You OK, Jo-Jo?' The taxi was moving.

'Rather taken aback,' said Jo-Jo with a strangled laugh. 'Honestly, James, I couldn't believe it. I'm so careful and . . .'

'Sure, but if you get robbed on the way home from a club it has to be a set-up. Either the people that run the club want their money back or one of their customers wants to relieve you of it. Chance scarcely comes into it.'

'James, I'm not certain you're correct about refusing to involve the police.'

Jim had been afraid of this. He carried on rubbing at a stubborn mark on his thigh. 'Oh?'

'Well one doesn't wish to encourage gun law on the streets of London. I did see the gun, you know.'

'OK, there was a gun. But don't you think it was there to frighten the driver and prevent him radio-ing for help? It's unlikely they intended to use it.'

Jo-Jo repeated the peculiar laugh. 'How I wish I could summon your confidence in the essential decency of the common criminal! I'm sorry, James, but I beg to differ. I shall report it once I get home.'

'How much did they take from you?'

'The whole damned lot, as a matter of fact.'

Roughly, he meant three thousand. Jim showed sympathy by a sharp indrawn breath.

Jo-Jo said: 'And you?'

162

'Around a tenth of that. Nothing like enough for me to consider hauling in the police. I guess I don't want it known I was taken for a sucker. They'd waste my time going over the details, they might give the press news of it and, like the driver said, the chance of catching anybody is round about nil. No thanks, I can do without the hassle. For three hundred, I'll write it off to experience.'

Jo-Jo wasn't falling for it. 'But, James, it isn't the cash, you know, it's the principle. One has to defend the odd principle now and then.'

'Ye-es, but it's my principle right now to keep a low profile.'

Jo-Jo cut short the argument to tell the driver: 'Over there, if you would, number 28.'

Once they'd dropped him off Jim said: 'We'll go on to Paddington now.'

The man smacked his forehead with his hand. 'I could have sworn you said Pimlico. Shows what that bit of excitement's done to my memory.'

'I changed my mind.'

At Paddington the driver reached beneath his seat and drew out the package Jim had entrusted to him outside the club. Ironic, he said: 'Bit of luck, that. Pity your mate wasn't so careful.' Jim unfolded the paper and peeled off a couple of fifties. 'Maybe I've been around more than he has.'

'I'd say so.' His eyes didn't stray to the cash, he was taking a long hard look at Jim. Jim knew he was the kind to swear he never forgot a face.

The driver said: 'They weren't interested in him, were they? He was a bonus. But I got the impression one of them knew you.'

Jim held the notes up in front of him. 'That was a misleading impression. But I expect it will fade.'

'I reckon it will.' He took the money.

At the station taxi rank Jim hired another cab to take him to Tubbs Road. Stefan had left a note on Jim's bed. *'That man called again today. Says he'll be round tomorrow, about seven.'*

Jim crumpled it into the wastebin and went to bed. He

was seeing Jane Logan the next evening, the detective would go unanswered once more.

During the night he woke, the wind beating the wail of the trains against his window. He lay staring up at the ceiling, trying to make his mind blank to allow sleep to fill the vacancy. But his mind ran on parallels: lying on his back in a field and feeling the vibration of the earth beneath him before the Jones County express came through, lying in the blistering sun on a beach noticing how the attack of surf on shore mimicked the rhythm of trains, and then a shadow falling over his face as Glenda in a floppy sun hat stopped by to say hi and promised to change his life, lying in a narrow metal bed and pretending not to hear the sobs of the man in the other one.

He shook off memories and went to stand by the window. The night was bright, Willesden junction a grey monochrome interrupted by darts of yellow from engine cabs, winks of red and green from signals. There was nobody out there, his view never showed him a human form.

Mail trains, hoppers, sliding through the night. Excursion. Escape. He ached with the need to be gone and the knowledge that he must stay. Soon, once the theft from J. and J. was cleared up, he'd cut free of Tubbs Road and his job and he'd find a place in the heart of London. That would make it easier with Jane Logan, and then . . . The schemes, the daydreams, ran on showing him how things could be, how easy, how comfortable.

Yet there was a disturbing element spoiling the fanciful flow, thrusting into his consciousness until he saw himself snarled in a net of confusion, making it worse as he tried to break free. Matthew Reynoldes, James B. Orlando, junior, O'Malley and the small-time crooks playing big time: they'd trapped him. All he'd ever wanted was to be free. He'd achieved rootlessness, but he was never free.

He took from his wardrobe the suit that had suffered in the hold-up on the taxi and he sponged and brushed it with exquisite care. Then he hung it up near the window to air, and he went back to bed. Daydreams merged into proper dreams and he saw again the damaged butterfly and Jane telling an elaborate story about its fate. And then she was laughing and when he looked again at the butterfly it had become a snowman, and she was laughing and laughing as it melted to nothing on the veranda of a summerhouse.

He understood when he woke that he distrusted and envied Jane. Her circle had accepted him with ease but with the same ease they'd reject him when he no longer amused them. For a little while their protection extended to him: as a foreigner, and no threat to their social standing, they'd let him into their world, and they'd sneer when he melted. There were differences that, for all his ingenuity, were unbridgeable. The trick, as he always reminded himself, was to fit in. With them he couldn't, except in the most superficial way.

They were dedicated to keeping the social boundaries in good repair. Static, they poured energy into keeping things the same, preventing flux. Without rigid group behaviour, they'd be sunk. And he, well, he constantly reinvented himself, cast off the anchors of Iowa and floated unhindered across a continent and an ocean. He'd never met anyone from his county, no one who claimed to have known him back there, and if he ever did he'd duck. Such loyalty was alien to him, yet Jane's sort extended it to unmet friends of friends. Born into a club, they took out life membership and paid their dues without questioning.

He trailed down to the North London line and caught a train to Acton. If not Jane, then what? Nothing came to mind, nothing practical or half-way possible. The hope of using Jane as an escape wouldn't die, it would take more than a dream and a pessimistic mood.

Eight

The sun tore into him as he came out on the step. He shaded his eyes with a brown hand. 'Al, hi!'

'You coming for a ride, Jim?'

Al Weedon leaned against the pick-up, a hat tilted back on his head. He was a year older than Jim, they were going through school together.

'Sure.' He reached for a hat on the nail by the door.

Al said: 'Gotta pick up some stuff at O'Kelly's. Won't take but five minutes.'

Jim hopped up into the cab.

Al nodded at blocks of gold, still in the windless afternoon. 'Looking good. They'll be cutting any time now.'

He drove past his father's farm and then they were skirting Jim's aunt's. Jim watched out for Maria but she wouldn't have been out in the heat of the day.

Al said: 'You reckon you'll get her place some day, when she's gone an' all?'

'Could be.' He liked the sensation of the air rushing by, drying the sweat on his face and the arm that rested on the open window.

'Don't sound like you're waiting on it.'

'She'll be around years yet.'

Al swung past a cart drawn by a flagging horse. 'I heard she was thinking it over.'

There was a clue in the way he said it. 'Your pa been making her offers, Al?'

'No new ones, not that I know about. He'd get a good spread, though, if she was ever minded to agree.'

Maria had married Jack who'd had his arm ripped off

by a thresher and died of a haemorrhage. There'd been no children. No man had persuaded Maria to the altar since.

Jim said: 'I know she doesn't always speak well of Pa, but she'd leave the land in the family. She won't sell, feeling the way she does.'

'What way's that?' Al added a gesture and Jim obeyed, feeling beneath his seat and dragging out a cardboard box. Coke cans rolled around in it. He opened one for Al, another for himself.

Jim wasn't willing to look dumb spouting Maria's stuff about good English stock. He fell back on something his mother said. 'Maria has a strong sense of family.'

Al laughed, an open-mouthed ha-ha type of laugh. Maria didn't care for the Weedons. They were honest, hard-working folk who took care to get themselves married in church but she felt superior. Jim couldn't see her selling to them.

He jumped down from the pick-up while Al combed his hair and went to do his bit of business at O'Kelly's. A dog ambled through the dust, tongue lolling, to sniff around Jim's boots. O'Kelly's store and gas station, a truck trundling up the dirt road, the dog, Al, O'Kelly and O'Kelly's daughter all in the store, a high blue sky, bunched trees, an ochre barn and a shimmering grain elevator: that was all the world held. It wasn't enough.

Al came over and tossed a box into the back. 'Should've come on in.'

'You don't need me hanging around.'

Al repeated the gaping laugh. 'Got her pa in there, her ma out the back. When do I ever get her to myself?'

Jim smiled. That wasn't the way Al Weedon talked in front of the other guys. They got into the cab. The clutch was slipping and they lurched towards the road. When they gained speed it was OK.

Jim said: 'Do you ever want to hit the highway, get right on out?'

'Oh sure, all the time.'

'Eighty-eight all the way to Chicago?'

Al whooped and tipped his hat an inch further. 'All the way!'

'We can do that.'

'Yeah. But I gotta get this engine fixed. Don't want to be stranded on some God-forsaken stretch.'

'Thought we'd take a limo.' He felt Al's eyes swivel towards him, testing his seriousness. 'Or a convertible. Did you see that film on television? Those guys cruising?'

'Sure, right across. And those *girls*. Everywhere they pitched up there were girls waiting in line for the pleasure of riding along. "Hi, there," and then you see them riding along.'

'California,' said Jim, explaining everything.

Al drove on until they came to a place where they could eat burgers and sit around and watch people come and go. When the heat was easing Al drove them back.

'You coming in, say hi to Rosanna?' They were near the track to the Weedons' farm.

'Not this time.'

Al changed down a gear and gathered speed as they passed the track.

The Weedons, Jim thought, were born with transparent panels in their skulls. You could see their brains working. Old man Weedon wanted Maria's place to add to his own farm. Rosanna, their only daughter, was being pushed at him because, as an only child, he'd one day have his father's land and probably Maria's. She was all right, Rosanna. Average plain but all right. They'd have stayed friends if he hadn't been scared off by what he read through those transparent panels.

Everyone around him was offering things he didn't want: Maria, his parents, the Weedons too, all of them. Nobody ever looked into his head to see what was going on there. They'd made up their minds what he wanted, but they were wrong.

His mother was fanning herself with a magazine and watching television. In another room his father was carving patterns in a leather belt. Jim ran upstairs, threw open his casement and watched light fading to darkness. From miles away he heard the faint troubling of the air. His skin prickled, anticipating that second when the engine rounded the hill.

Then his whole body was charged as it ripped through the tranquillity of the fields.

A cruise with Al Weedon in a limo? A joyride to Chicago in a convertible? No, when he left he was going by train and he was going alone.

In the fall three cataclysmic events happened. Maria died and left her land to his father. Jim fondled Rosanna and broke her heart. And he walked over the ploughed land to a place where he could jump the train.

The van keys were in his hand, he was half-way through the door when Eric Shaw curled round in his chair, capped the telephone receiver with his palm. 'Someone asking for Mr Rush.' He invested the words with a deal of malice.

'For me? Who is it?' Nobody had ever called him at work. Jim's heartbeat quickened. The police, he thought. After that fiasco with the shop-door bolts and the theft from the stock room, they'd done some checking and they had fresh questions. *Damn.*

Shaw said: 'Somebody's secretary, I should say.'

Jim reached for the receiver. Did the police use secretaries? 'Hi, this is Jim Rush.' Cautious, his voice betraying him.

Shaw, who discouraged staff from making or receiving personal calls at work, was pointedly not stirring from his desk and allowing this one to be private. Jim tweaked the telephone lead clear of Shaw's ledger, and moved round the desk, turning his back on him.

Down the line came a woman's chuckle. 'Jim? I must say I don't think much of your secretary. Gruff old body, isn't she?'

'Penny?'

'Yes, the one you don't give your home number to. I had to resort to the phone book and your shop. Lucky I remembered the name from the side of that awful old van you appeared in once.'

'Well, er . . .'

'Why am I bothering you like this? OK, I'll be quick. My mother's gone to stay with her sister for a week and I thought you might like to come round. Tonight, in fact.'

'Could we make it tomorrow instead?'

'Afraid not. I'm going to the cinema with a schoolfriend, and the day after that I'm . . .'

'OK, tonight's fine. About eight?'

'Great. See you. Bye.'

He tossed the lead back, replaced the receiver. He expected Shaw to pass a remark about girlfriends cluttering up a business line but he said nothing. He sat there, in his grubby old pinstripe and his tattered shirt collar. He looked a fool and he looked full of spite. Jim waggled the van keys at him and went out into the sunny yard.

During the morning he talked a woman into having a satellite dish fixed on the back of her house instead of the flank wall. Once the job was finished he rang Jane Logan's flat. She was at work but he didn't know the precise name of the gallery and he didn't have a number. He left a message on her machine to say that he wouldn't be able to take her to dinner after all.

The police were with Eric Shaw when he returned to the office. Daphne beckoned him as he entered the shop.

'Don't go in the office, Jim, they want to be private.'

Through the glass door he made out the heads of Shaw and the sergeant who'd come on the day the theft from the stock room had been discovered. They were either side of Shaw's desk. Shaw was doing the talking.

Daphne said: 'It's been an hour already. Whatever it is, they're being thorough about it. Well, that ought to suit our Eric, pernickety sod that he is.'

Then she switched on her businesslike air. 'I'd appreciate a telly delivered the other side of Acton. Do you mind, Jim?'

'No problem.'

Delivering equipment wasn't his responsibility and Shaw was fussy about who did what, but as the job list was in the office Jim couldn't find out what he was supposed to be doing.

'I'll explain to Eric when he comes out.'

'Don't worry, Daphne, I may be back before then.'

'Yes, I keep hoping to hear the click of handcuffs.'

Jim cocked an eyebrow.

'Wishful thinking,' she said. 'Gawd, wouldn't it be great if the law carted the old so-and-so away and left us to get on with running a shop?'

'Keep dreaming. Now, where's this telly?'

'In the stock room. I'll give you the keys.'

Nobody had tidied it after the burglary. Jim kicked empty boxes aside and hunted down the set that matched the details on Daphne's order form. It was near the window. For a moment he looked out on traffic grinding by, at sensible Victorian buildings above lurid shop fronts, at pedestrians scurrying along in thin summer clothes. He was going to miss all this, miss being part of something simple and straightforward, miss Daphne's commonsense, Shaw's bitchiness, the ordinary people who came in and out.

And Alex. Already he missed Alex, the streetwise kid with the swagger and the skin-tight jeans, the kid who wanted to put one over on Shaw but even when he was handed a ready-made plan made a mess of it.

Jim hoisted the television set. Stupid Alex. Oh, but wily too if the police were correct and he'd stolen the stock and played a trick with the bolts to lock Shaw out of his domain.

An idea came to him. He put the set down. From the landing he listened for sounds from below. The shop doorbell pinged, television sets continued their argument between children's programmes, chat shows and afternoon films. A man might do anything upstairs as long as he was quiet. So what had gone on up there?

With a surge of energy he attacked the boxes piled against the side wall, shifting them nearer the centre of the room. In his head was a vivid picture of a door, brown-painted like the rest of the room, and leading to the empty premises next door. Had J. and J. at one time rented the big room above the next shop as an additional store room? The pile of boxes diminished as he constructed a story so convincing that when the wall was revealed doorless he felt cheated.

He went through the second- and third-floor rooms. No doors there, either. And then on the top landing he spotted something that would do equally well. Wary of leaving evidence of his own presence, he decided not to test the theory.

What was it Penny Reynoldes had called it? The Locard principle? He curbed a smug smile, collected the television set, locked the stock room and went back to the shop.

That day he left work early on the pretext of going to discuss a possible satellite sale. Shaw, wearied by the hours spent with the police sergeant, paid scant attention to the excuse.

Stefan was in Jim's room. Jim was warned by a cool draught funnelling down the stair well from the attic window.

'Hi,' he said. 'What's happening out there?'

Stefan gave a start. The noise outside had prevented him hearing Jim's approach. 'Hello, Jim. I . . .'

They both stopped. Stefan's anxiety became guilt. And then Jim understood. Stefan wasn't wearing his familiar trousers with the baggy waistband and the escaping shirt, he'd put on a pair of good-quality lightweight trousers and a cotton jacket, Jim's own clothes, the ones ruined the night Matthew Reynoldes died.

Jim burst out laughing. 'It looks good. I wouldn't mind something like that myself.'

'It wasn't thieving, was it? I mean, you threw them away, didn't you? You didn't want them any more.'

'Sure, that's the way it was.'

He took two glasses from the shelf, opened a can of lager, shared it out. And he waited for the questions: why had the clothes been so wet, how had they been damaged?

Stefan drank the lager and watched the trains and was content without explanations. Jim shook his head. The boy was crazy. Well, not literally but he didn't react as other people did. He was limited. Yes, that was it. Narrow. Diminished. Limited. Simple problems, simple pleasures.

The clothes had been mended. Stefan had chosen to pay for that rather than acquire brand new ones, which he could have done because cheap clothing wasn't hard to come by.

The realization that Stefan had made that choice gave Jim a funny feeling. He'd been aware of Stefan's admiration but this was bordering on adulation. How far might Stefan's

gratitude for small services – form-filling, a little companion-
ship, shielding him from Geordie – stretch?

When he hurried for the Richmond train, Jim felt Stefan's
gaze on him. This was physically impossible, the attic
window at Tubbs Road showed the lines, an impression of
platforms and nothing of the streets. The sensation was
formed of guilt. He knew he was being silly, Stefan had
gained a better set of clothes and if Stefan was happy there
was no problem.

He told himself: 'Leave the guilt until the day you clear
out. That's going to hit him hard.'

The train was delayed. He caught a taxi from Richmond
station to Queens Road where Penny was filling in time
gossiping on the telephone. She opened the door to him and
went back to the telephone.

'Mmm,' she was saying. 'Well, you know how I feel about
that. Oh yes, *I* would. After all, it's your life, you've got to
make the decisions. Mmm. That's right.'

Jim went into the sitting room, out on to the lawn. He
pictured Matthew Reynoldes mowing the lawn, Matthew
Reynoldes planning to tack a balcony outside his bedroom
window, Matthew Reynoldes full of his own importance and
making life difficult for his wife and daughter. Then the other
pictures came crowding in, the ones that showed Reynoldes
lunging at Jim or Reynoldes lifeless by the riverside.

And yet it seemed long ago, years rather than weeks. Jim
had moved on, coming here dragged him back. It was like a
board game where he made stupendous advances and was
winning his way towards 'Freedom', but every so often a
card marked 'Penny' turned up and he'd be back near the
beginning.

'Gosh, you look glum, Jim. Something wrong?' Penny was
tripping across the grass to him.

'I'm fine.' He kissed her upturned face.

'How's the dog bite?' She took hold of his hand, looking
at the plaster.

'Coming along fine.'

'Good. Drink? Or shall we have one down by the river?'

'I like it here, and it's a novelty to have it to ourselves.'
He was nervous of bumping into Reynoldes's mistress again.

'All right. We'll stay.'

There was salad, cold salmon, peaches and white wine.
They ate outside, flitting from one topic to another. Beneath
the surface he was nudging her towards talking about the
police investigation. They'd loaded the dishwasher and were
locking up, ready for a walk in the park, before he got her
anywhere near it.

She was reaching for a bolt high on the back door when
she said: 'By the way, Daddy went into the park the evening
before he was found.'

'Oh?' He clicked the dishwasher control round and pressed
the button. Water rumbled into the machine.

'Yes, isn't that weird?'

Jim recalled one of her didactic speeches about forensic
evidence and asked whether an analysis of soil in the car
had indicated it.

'No, I don't think it was that.' She finished with the bolts
and the burglar alarm. 'There. Off we go.'

The Reynoldes's back gate took them into the park, to the
left of the road through it.

'Actually, I always feel the need of a dog if I'm to walk in
here,' she said. 'I'm incomplete without one when it comes
to healthy walks.'

'Then why don't you have one?'

'Daddy refused point blank. I pleaded, Mummy coaxed,
but he was adamant. No dogs, he hated the creatures. We'll
go over that way, we might see deer.'

The grass was brittle and scratchy on her sandalled feet.
She stopped to tease out the pieces that wriggled in under
her toes.

When she straightened, Jim said: 'You were going to
explain about your father being in the park.'

Ahead of them and a few degrees to the left was the stand
of trees that Reynoldes had forced him to enter.

'Oh yes. The thing is, they were seen up here. Daddy and
the man who got into his car on the hill.'

His scalp prickled. 'Who saw them?'

'Two people reported Daddy's car by the roundabout at the top of the hill. Apparently he was driving very fast and rather badly, that's why they noticed him. They watched him go through the park gates over there.'

'Did anybody see him after that?'

'No, or not that we know of yet. Maybe someone who was on holiday when the appeal was made will hear about it and go dashing off to the police station with a really crucial titbit.'

They were heading for the stand of trees. Jim manoeuvred to keep clear of them but each time Penny corrected their line. She was enthusing about the terribly helpful inspector.

'He told us there's one detail that wasn't in the appeal but the people by the roundabout referred to it. And therefore the police are certain they are talking about the identical car seen lower down the hill.'

'What was this detail?' His voice sounded tight, he covered it with throat clearing.

'The fair-haired young man wasn't in the front with Daddy, he was sitting in the back seat.'

She paused for dramatic effect and when he didn't respond she ran on: 'God, isn't it awful? There could have been a gun, or a knife maybe. Daddy could have been forced to drive up the hill, prevented from turning into Queens Road to get home and ordered into the park. The couple knew Daddy by sight and they both described him as looking strange, red and angry.'

'Did they say anything particular about the passenger?'

'Like what?'

'Anything to suggest he had a gun or a knife? I wondered where you got the idea your father was being threatened.'

'Jim, I told you – the passenger was in the back! People don't normally do that. And the state poor Daddy was in . . .'

He put an arm around her shoulders. She swung towards him, his arms encircled her.

'Take it easy, Penny.'

Her eyes were shining with tears. 'I'm sorry. It's awful to think what might have been happening to him.'

He brushed her face with a finger. 'I know, Penny, but it mightn't have been that way at all.'

She wriggled with impatience. 'Jim, that passenger hasn't come forward, has he? I can't help believing he was up to something really bad.'

The tears were on her eyelashes now. She pulled free and rubbed her fists into her eyes. Then she walked on. The stand of oakwood was close. Jim caught up with her.

Penny said, choked: 'I'm sorry. I'd better stop talking about it. I don't want to spoil our walk by snivelling.'

Quickly, before it was too late to seem natural, he said: 'Was there much else?'

'I'll tell you later, Jim.' She blew her nose. 'Now, if we're lucky we'll see the herd on the far side of these trees. That's where they were this afternoon, so one of the neighbours says.'

He hated it, walking with Penny Reynoldes through the wood where he and her father had grappled, and fighting to remember that the guilt was Reynoldes's and not his own.

They seemed destined to linger. Penny was pointing out tiny creatures, making him freeze as she studied them in the interval before they vanished into foliage or undergrowth.

She was like an alert golden cat, with her shining hair, her tanned skin, her athletic grace. She crouched to peer where a wren had sought cover. The creamy material of her dress hung from her shoulders. Jim saw the brown curve of her breasts, the edging of lace that gathered their weight and squeezed them together. Abruptly he stepped away from her. The wren was alerted by his movement. It churred, its wings beat air.

Penny was cross. 'Jim, you frightened her.'

'It was only a bird, for heaven's sake.'

She rose. 'Don't you want to see the deer? We needn't bother if you've changed your mind.' She had her head on one side like a toddler.

'I haven't. Let's find them.' But he knew he was behaving oddly, that she was perturbed by it.

'Jim, I don't understand why you're . . .'

'Come on.' He held out a hand to her. 'Show me your deer.'

Her hand was slim and strong, the cushions below the fingers marred with callouses caused by gripping tennis rackets. He played his fingers across her palm and began telling her a story about his life in America, lying to her.

She said: 'Shhh. What's that?'

'Where?'

Penny tipped her head towards the right, a gesture she trusted was imperceptible to wildlife. She whispered again: 'I saw something move.'

Jim relinquished her hand. Dreading it, knowing the inevitability of it, he saw her glide away, draw him on with a discreet wave of her hand held low. His heart ached with the urge to flee.

Penny sank to a squat. Her hand flapped to signal him to do the same, but he stood, looking over her head and round the tree she was using for cover.

He gave the hind a second's attention and then peered through the trees beyond it, picking out the exact place. He remembered the fist catching him off-guard, successive blows that he'd shied from returning because the man was older and less fit, and then the moment they'd closed and fallen. He remembered the sound of it: the tearing fabric, the snuffling and groaning. And he remembered the astonishing, alarming moment when he'd felt for a pulse that no longer beat.

His breath escaped in a sigh that sounded like boredom. The hind sprang from sight. Penny rounded on him.

'Did you have to do that?' She seemed about to say more but held back. Then: 'Why don't we cut across to the road and walk back that way?'

'I thought you were keen to see the herd of deer.'

'It doesn't matter. I can see them any time.' She strode ahead.

The hind had joined the herd. Seeing them would have taken Penny to the far side of the trees, making for the road was leading her to the scene of the fight. Again she paused for him to catch up. They were hidden from the road but could see cars coursing along in the deadening light of evening.

Jim was shocked to find himself enjoying the frisson of standing where he'd faced Reynoldes. She was looking over to the road. He took a pace or two until his back touched the trunk of the tree where Reynoldes had pinned him.

'Penny, you're doing it again, aren't you? Seeking clues in the ether.'

'I never found any on the riverbank, I don't suppose there'll be any on the road.'

'But we have to walk along the road anyway, to make sure?'

'Don't laugh at me.'

'I'm not laughing.'

He opened his arms to her. Her face was solemn and he realized he hadn't been warmed by the sunny Penny Reynoldes smile all evening. He caressed the fine cotton on her back, ran fingers down the knobby vertebrae until they disappeared beneath her belt. He pressed her to him, roused by the sweet scent of her skin.

He had an inclination to make love to her there, to overlay hideous memories with the tenderness of lovemaking. But he knew he wouldn't do it, that he wouldn't suggest it and she wouldn't let him. They only ever kissed. There'd never been a repetition of her eagerness in the car by the river, no other occasion of rejection. Matthew Reynoldes had been wrong in his accusation because Jim had never intended to seduce Penny.

She stirred and wisps of her hair tickled his cheek. He imagined a scene: Penny lying beneath him on the soft floor of the wood, looking at him with dreamy anticipation, opening her muscular brown legs for him.

Again she stirred, leaned back to look into his face. There was no dreaming surrender about her, she hadn't been thinking of him at all. She said: 'Let's go and check out the ether.'

He nodded, but he continued to hold her.

Penny squirmed, failed to free herself. He kissed her. Gravely she removed one of her gleaming hairs from his shoulder, not brushing it off but lifting it and holding it twirling between finger and thumb.

He was fashioning a joke when she said: 'They found a hair. On the back seat of Daddy's car they found a hair they think was left by the fair-haired young man.'

And then, as his grip tightened: 'Hey, don't crush me!' She giggled and raised her mouth to his.

'Another pub fight?' Detective Sergeant Boulter stared at the plaster on Jim's hand.

'No, a dog bite.' Jim was keeping him on the landing.

Boulter tutted, pretending sympathy. 'There are some dangerous animals around. What was it? Rottweiler?'

'Can we hurry this? I have got to get to work this morning.'

'Frightened of the boss? Doesn't sound your style, Jim.'

'I have to be there.'

'All right, all right. Five minutes, that'll do me. But not on the stairs where everybody can hear us. You wouldn't really want that, would you, Jim?'

Jim pushed open the door behind him, let Boulter follow him into the room. Boulter succeeded in appearing both to wrinkle his nose at the room's stuffiness and also to look down it in disdain.

'Bit of a rush this morning, was it? Burnt the toast, did we?'

Equally sarcastic Jim replied: 'I'll open the window while you make the bed.'

He threw up the sash. Outside the day was already hot, although the sun was a vague smog-brown presence. From the dusty country an express loped towards Euston.

Boulter had taken the chair near the window, leaving Jim to flatten out the bedclothes and sit on the end of the bed.

'Right,' said Jim, with exaggerated attention. 'Why are you here?'

Boulter was stringing it out. Jim was too tired to handle it well. He resorted to weary silence, waiting for the man to get to the point. *Any* point.

Boulter said: 'How about some coffee?'

Silence.

'I thought you were going to get some choccy biscuits for when I dropped in again.'

More silence.

'Of course, I can see you wouldn't actually look forward to my little visits, but even so, Jim, there's such a thing as hospitality.'

Jim looked at his watch. He was affecting the elegant unconcern perfected by Jane Logan's crowd, the air of policemen-are-so-tiresome-but-one-does-what-one-can.

Inside his head the fears jostled for supremacy. If he was lucky, Boulter was still harping on his activities on a Tuesday and a couple of Thursdays, in which case he was in the clear although proving it needn't be easy.

'All right,' repeated Boulter, dropping the nonsense. 'I'm here for you to tell me about your mate, Alex, and his fiddles over at J. and J. Electrical. Knew what was going on, did you?'

Jim let the languor conceal relief. 'Not a thing.'

'Didn't put ideas in the kid's head or anything?'

'Is he blaming me?'

'No. But Mr Eric Shaw isn't wholly convinced of your innocence.'

'Oh, him.'

'Don't underestimate him, Jim.'

He allowed a knowing smile. 'I don't. Believe me, I don't.'

Boulter's five minutes grew into half an hour. He concentrated on Alex, his opportunities and his culpability. Jim suffered only the token barb. At the end, Jim was pleased with the way it had gone. He hadn't incriminated Alex and he'd tossed in his personal doubts about Alex's responsibility for the raided stock room and the bolted doors.

'Stick around,' said Boulter, at the head of the stairs. 'I might be back, you never know. Not planning a holiday, are you?'

'I'll be around.'

Jim shut the door. The next train to Acton wasn't due, this gave him time to make a mug of coffee. While the kettle boiled he examined his appearance in the mirror. A tightness around the eyes, a paleness of the skin, suggested worry and a late night. He combed his hair, buffed his shoes again.

Relax, he thought, Boulter's way off the mark. He hasn't made any of the links and probably never will. This isn't the kind of trouble you ought to meet half-way, not if it leads to you going around looking scared to death. But after that he warned himself that it wasn't merely Boulter interested in him, it was also the young policeman who Stefan said had called at the house twice.

He drank the coffee at the open window, too preoccupied to take notice of engine types or variations in rolling stock. He'd always run, it wasn't in his nature not to and he'd learned it was a mistake. Chicago, San Francisco, New York. He'd run.

A voice called out. 'Is that you, Jim?'

'Come on up, Stefan.' He read his watch again. He could spare a couple of minutes. Jim beckoned Stefan in.

'It's this,' said Stefan. 'They want me to fill another one in.' He showed Jim the latest form from the DHSS.

Jim scanned it. 'That'll keep until tonight. I don't have time right now.'

Stefan reached into the pocket of the jacket that used to be Jim's. 'The postman brought this too.'

A hand-written envelope addressed to Jim. 'Thanks, Stefan.'

'Can I . . . er . . .'

'Sure, you can borrow my window. But I have to go now. See you later, Stefan.' Jim put the form on the table and left.

His working day was safely dull, the only remarkable aspect Eric Shaw's confusion. Shaw's decision-making facility seemed stripped from him. His pen hovered above sheets of paper and wrote nothing. He was hesitant during telephone calls. And he didn't resist when Jim consulted staff records in a file that was none of his business.

Jim wanted Alex's telephone number. The letter Stefan had handed him was a frustrated plea from Alex who said he couldn't keep calling at Tubbs Road on the off-chance and begged Jim to be there the following evening because it was urgent they talk about the allegations the police and Eric

Shaw were making about him. He didn't call them allegations, he said they were lies.

Jim wanted to dissuade Alex from going to Tubbs Road and to reassure him with an account of his own conversation with Boulter. But Alex had no number. Jim resigned himself to waiting in next day.

Meanwhile he had to see Jane Logan and make up for his neglect. She was self-mocking when he rang her.

'James, would you believe I forgot to check my machine? I was showered and changed before I discovered my doom.'

'Oh, Jane, I'm really sorry.'

'No, it was my fault. Besides I rang Jeremy and Lucinda and said I was all dressed up with nowhere to go. The three of us went over to see Charles. You missed a wonderful time.'

'This evening then?'

'Make it nine. We're having a private view at the gallery. The usual frightful affair but I have to be there. I'd invite you but I'd prefer you to be my excuse for a fast getaway. Do go to the flat, James. I'll tell the porter to let you in.'

He agreed. He always agreed with her.

Her sleek, slender darkness, the sexy glimmer in her eye, were in stark contrast to Penny. Jim flipped through a folder of Jane's photographs while he waited for her to arrive at the flat. Jane skiing, Jane dancing, Jane sunbathing. And always Jane with friends.

The telephone rang. He waited for the machine to answer but after four rings he decided it could be Jane calling him. He took the call.

'Hi, this is Jane Logan's phone. She isn't here right now.'

An accusatory female voice asked: 'Who *is* that?'

'James Rush. She should be along any time. Would you care to leave a message?'

'Just to let her know I called. Tell her it's Camilla, please.'

The name jolted like an electric shock. She was gone before he could fish for details about whether she was in London or France. *Camilla* and he hadn't . . .

Jane's key turned in the lock. 'James? So sorry, I've been aeons.'

She kicked off her shoes and padded over the Persian rug to slide her arms around him. *'What* an evening.'

He kissed her. 'Busy?'

Disentangling herself, she collected the discarded shoes. 'Tremendously busy.'

She was on her way to the bedroom, saying: 'I'll be two minutes, I promise.'

'I didn't think people bought at viewings. I thought the general idea was to gossip and get drunk.'

'It is, and they didn't buy. What kept me busy was canvassing for someone to hold the fort while I take off for the Caribbean for a couple of months.'

There was a gilded mirror on her sitting-room wall. He could see her reflected in it, ripping off an elaborate silk jacket. He clenched his teeth lest she catch his reflection and notice dismay. As Camilla was becoming reality, so Jane was disappearing and it was Jane who was his lifeline.

His words were calm though. 'How soon do you take off?'

'End of the week, God willing. We hatched the plot over at Charles's last night.'

She trotted out the names of half a dozen friends, several familiar to him. They were all going. Then she went into the bathroom, he heard water running. She re-emerged rubbing her face and neck with a towel.

'Which island?' he asked.

'St Elena.'

She slid her arms into a frothy blouse, made a wiggling movement as she worked her feet into the lower, strappy shoes, and came through to join him.

'It's a speck on the map,' she said. 'You're excused from recognizing it. A cousin of Jo-Jo owns it. Of course, Jo-Jo won't be there. No casino.'

She looped her arm through his. 'Supper, before I faint.'

That night he stayed at her flat, lying awake long after they'd made love and listening to traffic droning in the main road a couple of streets away. Her breath on his arm was light, untroubled. Now that the pleasurable effects of alcohol were wearing off, he was bitter and humiliated.

'You're a fool,' he mouthed into the darkness. 'You heard

that snowman conversation, you knew she didn't want you in her life for long. How could you have kidded yourself that *you* were going to use *her*?'

And the words were repeated in his brain: *A beautiful stud. A beautiful stud.*

He sighed. She pressed closer, clinging. He clenched his eyes and tried to think of the best way ahead, after the weekend when Jane Logan and her friends dropped him.

Over breakfast she raised her face from the morning paper and teased him. 'Why so wistful, James?'

'Two months is a long time.'

'Will you miss me?'

She received the yes she required.

'Good,' she said. 'I'd hate to go and not be missed.'

After that she made a flurry about being late. 'As I'm going to take two months' leave of absence, I have to put on a bit of a show until the end of the week.'

Amusing, but he kept a straight face. Her working day didn't begin earlier than 10.30 and it was usually over by 5.00. Nothing he'd heard suggested she had much to do in between, except lunch.

Jane leaned over and kissed him where he sat. 'There's the paper, I've hardly creased it. Stay as long as you like, my sweet, but do put the catch down on the lock when you go out.'

He poured himself more coffee and opened the paper, but he couldn't keep his mind on international crises or political posturings. His own trouble crowded out all else. And as if there weren't already enough of it, on page two he found a succinct paragraph about Kent police charging people in connection with an international car-theft ring. The only vehicle singled out for mention was a one-year-old Bentley, a hire car.

Jim rang J. and J. and cried off with a stomach upset. He couldn't face leaving the security of the flat, not with O'Malley and his friends out there baying for his blood. All morning he hung around, failing to reconstruct his future. He could get no further than a rough plan to call at Tubbs Road, collect the hidden money, swear Stefan to secrecy, and return to Kensington. Jane's flat was his only refuge.

He squandered the afternoon in bookshops and a cinema. Coming out of the cinema, blinking against the light, he heard his name spoken with astonishment. A beaming girl, a haze of blonde hair, swam into focus. His own amazement was equal to hers.

Penny said: 'This is incredible, it's the second time we've met around here.'

And he agreed although what was amazing him was the woman who stood next to Penny, the auburn-haired woman he'd seen with Matthew Reynoldes.

Penny was saying: 'This is Sarah, from school. Do you remember, Jim? You met her in the café in Richmond once.'

She meant the girl on her other side. Jim nodded in acknowledgement of Sarah.

'And this,' Penny ran on, 'is Jennifer. We're sisters.'

'Sisters?'

Penny was loving seeing him mystified. '*Half*-sisters,' she said. 'Daddy was married before he met Mummy. Jennifer lives over the river from us, in Twickenham.'

His eyes met Jennifer Blake's. She wasn't smiling, not at all. She was greedy with interest.

Penny was saying: 'I've told Jennifer all about you, Jim.' She was oblivious of their reaction to each other.

He excused himself, spotting a cab dropping passengers at the queue for the next showing. 'I'll call you, Penny.'

As the cab drew away, she was obscured by the press of people on the pavement. The driver slid back the dividing glass. 'Where to?'

'Willesden. Tubbs Road.'

'Off Harlesden High Street? By the beige and white church?'

'The Church of God the Prophet. You've got it.'

They'd travelled a couple of miles before Jim noticed a taxi tailing them. He asked the driver to stop for him to go into a newsagent's. From the corner of his eye he registered the other cab slew into the kerbside a hundred yards back. When he returned, carrying an evening paper, it was waiting there. It moved off as his cab did.

Jim said: 'I'd like to go to Chiswick instead.'

The driver's shoulders hunched. 'Anywhere you say.'

'By the river. There's a pub down there.'

'There are two. The Dove? The Old Ship?'

'The Old Ship.'

Eventually the driver realized they were being pursued. Jim opened the newspaper and sought details of the car-ring charges. Nothing. But as he folded the paper again a late paragraph leaped out. A London man had been badly injured by a parcel bomb delivered to his flat by a figure in motorcycle gear. The flat was in Kentish Town. The man's name was Max Minter.

Jim recreated the scene: houses divided into flats, a path, an entryphone he'd used to trick another occupant into opening the street door, his own words to the thugs who'd driven him there: 'Top floor.' He'd read Max Minter by the bell for the top flat, but he was prepared to believe O'Malley's cronies hadn't bothered or else had taken it for granted it was an alias for Jim Rush.

The taxi jerked as the handbrake came on. Jim stepped down, feeling for cash. The river was high, the air humid and the taxi's diesel fumes nauseating. Jim took up position by the chest-high wall and waited. Lazy waves were slapping against stone. A college team was sculling on the far side, the cox's voice clear over the water. Jim heard a second taxi draw up and both of them move off. When they'd gone, there were only her footsteps, clack-clacking to meet him.

'Hello, Jennifer.' He treated her to the smile that helped him out of scrapes. 'I guess you're chasing me around town.'

She came to a halt a yard or two away. 'Who the hell *are* you?'

'Penny's told you.'

A snort. 'You've fooled Penny, but your charm is wasted on me. I recognize you, you know. You came to my house.'

He waited for her to go on. He wanted the measure of what she knew.

She said: 'You don't own that business in Acton. I telephoned and inquired.'

He raised a laconic eyebrow. His silence was bothering her, making her gush.

'Penny told me the name of it and I knew it was familiar, but it took me days to realize why. Then it clicked. There was a van with that name on it in the car park when my father gave me a lift back to Richmond after work. My God, I just can't believe your cheek. You were spying on us, on Daddy and me.'

She'd alarmed herself, despite her anger and her jubilation at having pinned him down. She looked about her. A second crew was going downriver, an elderly man and his spaniel were further along The Mall, but there was no one close except Jim. She looked once more at the water.

He put on his Southern drawl, derisive. 'My, you're getting real tense.'

Her face was changing, reminiscent of Matthew Reynoldes's now that her temper was surging out of control. 'Why were you spying?'

'You're making something out of nothing at all.'

'Don't patronize me.' She bit off the rest, clamped her lips for a moment, then: 'You're to keep clear of Penny and the rest of my family, or . . .'

'Or what? Doesn't Penny have a say in this?'

'She's a child. Look, if you've got any decency you'll vanish from our lives as suddenly as you arrived. Am I making myself clear?'

Jim lounged against the wall. 'Sure.'

Once more she tried, emphatic, demanding. And once more he heard her out without rising to her bait. And then the rage collapsed and she moaned and ran her hands through her thick auburn hair.

'Look, you know what happened to our father. You know the stress we're under, not being sure whether he was murdered. Yes, all right, I'm being protective about Penny. But someone has to be. Her mother's . . . well, her mother can't cope. Not at the moment, especially. Please will you see it this way: having you around isn't helping Penny.'

Irony tinged his words. 'I'm touched by the sisterly devotion. I guess you want my solemn promise on this.'

'No. No promises. I wouldn't trust any promise you made.'

'Wow!' He clapped a hand over his heart as though her words had inflicted a mortal wound. He detected cunning in her eyes.

'Look,' he said, teasing her with mimicry of her middle-class Englishness, 'the pub is open, the friend I'm meeting isn't here yet and I'd like to buy you a drink, Jennifer.'

The offer caught her off-balance. 'Oh . . . er . . . No, I don't think so.'

He moved towards the pub. 'Something to occupy you until you can get a cab. Come on, Jennifer.'

Doubtful, she went.

Jim ordered their drinks, and set hers in front of her at a table outside the front door where there was a good river view.

'Where would you like the cab to take you?' he asked.

She said Kensington because she had to meet Penny and Sarah when the film finished. 'We came over in my car. I dumped it five minutes from the cinema.'

'Don't move, I won't be long.'

He knew she watched his back as he walked inside and asked for the telephone. 'Around fifteen minutes,' he said when he came out. 'Heavy traffic today.'

'Out there too.'

On the river the scullers had been joined by a cruise boat and three launches as well as a boy paddling a kayak. Jim and Jennifer Blake kept to the safe subject of the river. He timed it so that he finished his drink ahead of her, offered a refill she declined, and rose to fetch his own. While the barman poured, Jim went towards a door marked Gentlemen.

He didn't go in there. He made for the pub's rear access, and went rapidly up a side street to the main road. Near the Hogarth roundabout he flagged down a taxi.

He backed her to realize he'd escaped her, that he'd only pretended to summon her cab, and he was convinced she'd force Penny to make the deductions that Penny had never made. He had to clear out of Tubbs Road before she winkled his home address from someone at J. and J.

No more decisions, other people were making them for him. No more scheming, nothing to do but go. Run away, from O'Malley and the men who'd attacked Max Minter by mistake. Run away, from the hotel and the stores that had bills for Orlando. Run away, from Eric Shaw and his cruel deviousness. Run away. Run. *Run*.

Jim chased down the passage at Tubbs Road, noting the unusual fact of the open back door and Geordie in the lobby clearing the stacks of newspapers. Good, Geordie needn't see him. A door slammed, caught by the draught. Jim took the stairs two at a time, slipped and jarred his shoulder against the wall.

His door was open, his window too, but Stefan wasn't there. Jim wrenched his bag from beneath the bed, lifted the neatly arranged clothes from the wardrobe and folded them into the bag. He owned little. Very, very little. The important item was in Stefan's room.

He hid the packed bag and ran down a flight, to inveigle Stefan up to watch the trains while he retrieved the hidden cash. But as he neared the bottom of the flight Stefan's door flew open and Stefan shot out, stumbling in his haste to get to the ground floor. In a split second Jim had spotted a man in the room, had thrust himself out of sight and was retreating to the attic.

Instinct took him to the window because there'd been no crash of the front door, nothing but Stefan's thundering steps and then a man charging after him, shouting: 'Hey, where do you think you're going?'

Stefan was in the scrap of garden, trapped by high walls. Jim saw him fling a terrified look towards the back door and then gather his courage.

Stefan scaled the rear wall, disappeared, came into view a few feet further on. Jim grabbed the window frame, leaned out screaming for Stefan to stop.

'You'll get killed. Come back. For Chrissakes come back, Stefan.'

But the trains blotted out the warning. Stefan ran on. He paused once and let a slow-moving goods train roll by.

'Stefan! Come back.' The words hurt Jim's throat and were wasted on the air. Stefan didn't even *look* back. Once the goods train was past, he started off again.

Jim moaned. There were electric lines out there, one careless footing and . . . For the third time he heard his own urgent cry.

Then, to the left, he saw a flash of movement. A flyer from Euston was streaking over the junction. And he saw that Stefan hadn't seen, was ploughing on, deafened by other trains sliding up to the platforms away on his right, chanting over the glinting rails. Jim's mouth was open but soundless. The hands locked on the window frame were trembling, powerless.

At the last, something alerted Stefan, a murmur on the line or an intimation of peril. He wavered. Jim dared to breathe. But then Stefan skipped forward and the train was where he had been.

The express screamed away, the noise bursting in Jim's skull. When it was gone he saw the running figure in the pale cotton jacket, and it was as though it were a wish, a creation of his willpower, and that he was not really seeing a man there because it was incredible that Stefan had cleared the track unscathed.

Stefan was far out in the junction and running. He looked around, slowed, came to a stop. Another express was tearing towards him but this time he was prepared for it. He stood still to let it go by.

Stefan didn't know about the draught and the suck until it drew his body into the shiny blur of the wheels and ground it. And ground it.

The train sped on. When it had gone there was no one on the tracks, only what seemed to be twisted rags of no distinct colour. A pair of crows floated down to perch beside the rags.

Jim's hands fell from the window frame. Gorge rose in his throat and he reached the washbasin in time to vomit. After, he realized there was someone in the room with him. Geordie.

'Stupid sod,' said Geordie in the direction of the window. 'Bloody dangerous game, that was.'

Stupefied, Jim lashed out. 'He didn't understand. Don't you see, even after this? Stefan didn't understand anything, not ever.'

He choked off his words, afraid of his own passion. He wished he were capable of explaining that Stefan was inexperienced, that his failing was a failure to accrue experience. But he knew the effort would be wasted. Unwilling to give up, though, he tried to get out a few less antagonistic words. His voice cracked, denying him. There was a lump in his throat, painful and unmanning.

He managed one bleak line. 'He was the kid that never got to play with the train set.'

And then he was crying, for the pity of it, the sheer unutterable pity of it. Jim scrubbed at the tears. He turned from Geordie's unsolicitous gaze and he leaned against the wall, head on his forearm and his shirtsleeve soaking up the tears. It was all flowing from him, the misery and the pain.

When he raised his head, in a few minutes, Geordie had gone and Detective Sergeant Boulter stood in his place, quizzical. Boulter said: 'Friend of yours, was he, Jim?'

'Not exactly, but I was his.' He felt for a handkerchief, his voice thick.

'Bit of an oddball by all accounts.'

'Whose accounts?' Jim blew his nose.

'Mine, if you like. I wanted to know where he got that outfit he was wearing and rather than let me in on the name of his tailor he dives under an InterCity.'

There was a peculiar lightness in Jim's head. He dropped on to the chair by the window. His movement stirred the DHSS form lying on the tabletop beside it. 'What was so interesting about those old clothes? Stefan always dressed in what Oxfam couldn't sell.'

Boulter sat on the edge of the bed and cracked his fingers, looking sideways at Jim. 'How long had he had that gear?'

An irritated shake of the head. 'I don't know.'

Boulter said: 'He took it to a dry cleaner's in Willesden and had them fix damage and shorten the trousers. The manageress of the place told us that, your mate didn't.'

Jim adopted his bewildered expression. 'Sorry, I can't seem to follow what a dry cleaner's has got to do with what happened out there just now.'

'Simple, Jim. We're looking for a man who was dressed in similar clothes in Richmond on the night a man was murdered there. The clothes were damaged and very wet. And the woman at the dry cleaner's couldn't help remembering young Stefan taking her his ripped-up jacket and trousers, both of which were distinctly damp and whiffy.'

Jim thrust aside the terrifying suspicion that Stefan had been shielding him. He said: 'If the guy hadn't killed himself your story would be funny. *Stefan* in Richmond, involved in murder? Oh, come on. You must be deep in the bottom of the barrel if you can't come up with a better suspect than Stefan.'

Boulter said: 'You're right, I expect you are, Jim. But nobody accused Stefan of murder. All I wanted to know was whose clothes they used to be.'

He stood up and looked out of the window. 'We'll probably never know now.' Then he sighed and took the few steps to the open door, pausing on the landing to say: 'See you in court, then, Jim?'

The remark caught Jim unguarded. Boulter's smirk showed he'd enjoyed the flicker of uncertainty in Jim's face. Boulter said: 'The coroner's court, I mean, of course. You're the best witness we've got, aren't you?'

Alex came, as he'd written to say he would. Jim had forgotten. He was on the front path, shutting Tubbs Road out of his life for ever, when suddenly there was Alex.

'What's up?' said Alex.

'One of the guys at the house got killed.'

'Bloody hell,' said Alex. 'Not that young one who opened the door when I came round before?'

'That's the one.'

'Bloody hell,' repeated Alex. 'Car, was it?'

'He went under a train. Can we go and get a beer some-where?'

Alex was staring at the house, imagining heaven knows what. Jim said: 'He's not there.' A shudder. 'He's not any-where.' The picture of the bundle of rags and the crows refused to fade.

'You look like you need that drink.'

'There's a pub this way.'

They walked down Tubbs Road. Understanding dawned. 'I bet you saw it.'

'Alex, do you mind? I don't want to deal with that right now.'

'All right.' Disappointed, he walked without a word.

They sat in the pub and downed a couple of beers. Jim was half-listening to Alex's injured innocence at being accused of a crime he didn't commit in addition to the one he did. It was always the unfair accusations that stung.

In Jim's head a small voice was offering advice. 'You shouldn't be here. You've got to lose yourself, or someone's going to find you, and that's for sure. Time's running out. And you aren't doing Alex any favours, you have nothing for him. Not now, that's over. Like a lot of things this summer, you've come to the end of it.'

'Jim! You're not listening, are you? I want you to tell me what the fuck I do about Eric Shaw and you're going all feeble on me.'

Jim drank an inch of warm beer. 'I'll tell you what I'd do if they were fingering me for bolting the doors and magicking away the contents of the stock room.'

Alex leaned over the stained table until his nose was close to Jim's. 'What?'

'I'd ask why Eric spends time in the office in the evenings going through the books. And I'd ask where you get to if you climb up on that old gas stove on the top landing and push open the loft trap above it. It's my guess the loft runs through to the next building.'

'You been up there?'

'Not through that trap but there are dusty fingerprints on it so it sure looks like someone has.'

'The next building's empty, right?'

'Maybe the back door to it has been forced for the gear to be carried out that way.'

Alex brightened, but momentarily. 'What if it hasn't, though?'

'I'd want to know if anyone had borrowed the estate agents' keys recently. Anyone who does that has an opportunity to have duplicates cut.'

'Anyone name of Eric Shaw in particular?'

'In particular.'

Alex punched him on the arm. 'You're a bloody marvel. Fancy old Shaw . . . But why would he? I mean, it's his job on the line, he's always on about J. and J. being so wonderful, why would he want to go nicking the stock?'

Jim knocked back the rest of his drink. 'I have a train to catch.'

'Oh, come on. Why would he?'

'Alex, I've given you questions, not answers. You ask the questions and let the police get the answers. OK?'

'But if you think Eric might have done it, you've got to have an idea why.'

Jim gave an open-handed shrug. 'Gambling? Not drink, that would show. I'd bet on gambling. He has a reasonable job, but look how he dresses. Yes, I'd go for gambling.' He picked up his bag. 'Take care, Alex. And keep my name out of it.' Jim left him finishing his beer.

He took a taxi on the final stage of the journey to Kensington.

Traffic was heavy, crawling and stopping, crawling some more. That was how he came to notice the poster, an approximation of his own face outside a police station.

The drawing wasn't grotesque, they hadn't falsified it with staring eyes or a sinister twist to the mouth. It was an impression of a twenty-five-year-old male with regular features and fair hair, not sufficiently accurate for a stranger to tap him on the shoulder in the street, yet the people who knew him would be reminded of Jim Rush.

The taxi driver was talking over his shoulder about the traffic jam, pedestrians were zig-zagging between stationary cars. Any moment a face might look into his, realize his was echoed on the poster. He didn't read the words, apart from WANTED and MURDER. He bowed his head and rummaged in his bag. Beneath the clothes were the bank notes he'd rescued from Stefan's room while Detective Sergeant Boulter was outside radioing his colleagues about the accident and Geordie was occupied watching Boulter using the radio.

Jim paid off the cab some streets from Jane's flat. That way, if drivers were asked questions, the answers would be vague. He sounded cheery when the porter let him in. In the mirror in the lift he straightened his jacket, swept a hand over his hair.

Jane was happy. She held his face between her palms and kissed him, the way she might kiss a child.

'James, you look irresistibly beautiful. What have you been doing since this morning? Not making love to another woman, I hope.'

She was obliging him to laugh at himself. She said: 'Well, whatever it was, it was rather exciting. You have a positively pink glow.'

He didn't know what he was saying in reply, just words, filling in with words the way he always had to while his mind sought avenues and escapes. She eyed his bag.

'That looks terribly like an attempt to move in on me.'

Jim grabbed the opening. 'Now don't panic, you don't have to agree to it at all. But I just quit the Pimlico place.'

'Give me one good reason why I should rescue you from booking into a hotel?'

'Easy. You like having me around.'

'True. One night, James, no more. Then my sister and her friend come to stay. They are borrowing the flat while I go away.'

She suggested he dumped the bag in the bedroom. 'What happened over at Pimlico?'

'Other people had a claim. They arrived early and I made way for them. How are the Caribbean plans progressing?'

'Flight's arranged. And Cassie, bless her, has been coaxed into baby-sitting my job until I get back. The truth is, she isn't doing it entirely as a favour to an old school friend.

She's soft on Rupert who owns the gallery and if she doesn't get him into bed by the time I come home, she'll be distraught.'

There was much more of this. Over supper in a local restaurant Jane scattered snippets about the manoeuvrings of her friends. He knew the scene well enough to contribute the occasional witty observation. Tension surfaced once they returned to the flat.

Jane pulled away from his embrace. 'James, there's something I ought to discuss with you.'

This was surprising, she always initiated their lovemaking. She said: 'There's talk. It's troubling me a little.'

'What kind of talk?'

'Promise me you won't get furious.'

'When have you ever known me furious?'

'Well, Jo-Jo is saying strange things, about the pair of you being held up on the way home from a club.'

'Oh, that. It was no big deal, no one was hurt.'

'James, he's saying the men who did it knew you. And that he was robbed but you weren't.'

'That's not the way it was. They took what I had on me.'

'But he says you'd given most of it to the driver for safekeeping. Jo-Jo believes you knew that hold-up was going to take place, and that's why you wanted to talk him out of going to the police.'

'The guy's sore because he lost a packet.'

Jane was the other side of the room, putting as much space as possible between them. 'Honestly, I don't think that's it. Jo-Jo loses money as a matter of habit, we both know that. He's convinced himself you knew.'

'He's wrong!'

He needed a brilliant answer to Jo-Jo, not a querulous response, but he felt drained of ideas. Oh what did it matter? They'd all prefer to believe Jo-Jo anyway. He asked: 'Who's he told?'

She named people close to Jo-Jo.

'He's wrong, Jane.'

'That's what I told him. I forbade him to repeat it.'

'You did?'

She came towards him, a ghost of a smile at her lips. Her voice was a whisper. 'James, you have to be careful.'

His skin was tingling before ever she touched him. He drew her on to the sofa beside him. He had no reply for her.

She said: 'I've been known to invent hay fever for you, but I'm afraid that season is past.'

Her body was warm and heavy against his, and he was afraid she could feel how his was disintegrating, how the revelation of her knowledge was destroying him utterly. He ran a tongue over his lips and tried to organize thoughts, to form a sentence.

Jane leaned away from him, stretched a hand and pressed a switch on her answering machine. There was the whirr of a tape rewinding and then he heard his conversation with Camilla. He was hot with shame.

Jane switched off the machine and got up. 'If one doesn't answer fast enough, the machine is activated and records anyway.'

This is it, he thought. This is where everything ends. She's been playing me along all evening, ever since yesterday when she discovered that message. She's the lifeline and she's cutting it.

Jane said. 'Brandy?'

He cleared his throat. 'Er . . . please.'

She poured two glasses, then stood on her magic carpet looking down on him with her cheeky grin, the one he'd liked the first time they'd met, in the nightclub when she'd owned up to stealing his drink.

'Well, James.'

'I forgot to give you the message.'

'Careless,' she said. And cradled her glass in her hands and continued to look down at him.

Might as well get it over, he thought. At least she was leaving him the opportunity to speak the words first. He set his glass down. 'I guess I'd better find that hotel we talked about.'

'It's far too late, James. You can't leave now.'

He nearly missed her ambiguity.

Jane said, in her negligent manner: 'I was rather hoping you could be persuaded to come to St Elena.'

Stupidly he echoed: 'To St Elena?'

'If you're not too busy, of course. If you don't have to dash back to Connecticut. Or New York.'

'There'll be a few calls to make, but nothing I can't take care of.'

She raised her glass to him. 'To St Elena then.' And after she'd sipped: 'I don't guarantee what it'll be like. It's not exactly the Garden of Eden. But we both enjoy a risk, don't we?'

The rug shimmered, the colours grew intensely vivid. Jim heard himself talking, his words flowing, inventing, covering reality, the way he always had and always did and would do for the rest of his life.